FATTY
LIVER DIET
COOKBOOK

Healthy Food Menus

Healthy Food Menus

Chapter 4.

Breakfast Recipes

Chapter 5.

Grains

Chapter 6.

Lunch Recipes

Chapter 7.

Dinner Recipes

Chapter 8.

Vegetables

Chapter 9.

Salads

Chapter 10.

Juices and Smoothies

Introduction

Introduction Fatty liver, which is also known as steatohepatitis, is one of the most common complications of obesity. This condition is typified by increased fat accumulation within the liver cells resulting in an inability to effectively process fats. The fatty infiltration leads to inflammation and damages hepatic cells. The excessive accumulation of fat presumably occurs as a consequence of the elevated fatty acid levels within the blood plasma. This condition is considered dangerous as it may lead to non-alcoholic steatohepatitis (NASH) which can cause cirrhosis, liver failure, and even liver cancer.

This type of fat deposit within the liver is also known as Non-Alcoholic Fatty Liver Disease (NAFLD). The main causes of this condition are obesity and diabetes and fatty deposits can occur in other parts of the body too like the heart, pancreas and buttocks. It is a common disease that occurs when excess fat builds up in liver cells causing inflammation.

The fatty liver shows numerous signs and symptoms however the main one is fatigue along with an increase in the size of the abdomen. The patient might experience feeling light-headed, headache and shakiness. The skin might appear pale, and yellowish along with jaundice. These conditions lead to an increased risk of diabetes, stroke, cardiovascular disease and sleep apnea.

The condition mostly occurs when excess fat is deposited within the liver cells which is due to obesity and hypertension. Some of the other risk factors include diabetes mellitus, excessive alcohol consumption and viral hepatitis.

A blood test that determines the body's number of triglycerides is used to make the diagnosis. If the triglyceride level is found to be elevated then this may indicate the presence of fatty liver. The liver biopsy is taken which reveals the location, amount and volume of fat in the patient's body. Fatty liver can be treated easily with diet and exercise to reduce weight.

Fatty liver can be treated as long as it is caught in time, it may also be prevented by following a healthy diet and leading an active lifestyle thereby controlling weight gain or obesity. Some of the treatment options include dieting, exercise, and an anti-bacterial drug called trimethoprim.

NASH is a liver complication of NAFLD caused by chronic inflammation and excessive fat deposits in liver cells. NASH is characterized by an increased fatty acid content in the blood plasma that leads to higher levels of triglycerides (TG). NASH is found more in women than men. When the presence of NASH increases, this can result in cirrhosis which can cause severe health problems. Complications like Type 2 diabetes (often referred to as "adult-onset" diabetes), high blood pressure, heart disease and even cancer. Along with the aforementioned symptoms, patients may also suffer from gastrointestinal issues due to inflamed liver.

It is essential to avoid the risk factors of NASH, which include obesity and alcohol consumption. An healthy lifestyle through diet and exercise is also key. Decreasing fat intake and increasing fiber intake must be a priority if symptoms occur. An increase in exercise and a decrease in alcohol consumption can be helpful.

People suffering from NAFLD often have an increased risk of getting engaged in unhealthy lifestyles like smoking and excessive alcohol consumption for the rest of their lives. These people have more chances of developing Type 2 diabetes. Taking care of the condition is necessary to avoid its complications later in life. Lifestyle changes can help with NAFLD/NASH such as a healthy diet, exercising, not smoking, and moderate alcohol consumption.

Chapter 1. How Fatty Liver Develop

The days when fatty liver disease was attributed solely to high alcohol consumption are long gone. Alcoholic fatty liver is caused by the breakdown product acetaldehyde. The human body gets along well with this substance in smaller quantities and breaks it down again within several hours. If you regularly add large amounts of alcohol to the body, liver tissue will break down over time, as the acetaldehyde cannot be broken down quickly enough by the liver. Additionally, there is an oxygen deficiency, which affects how fat is metabolized and causes small droplets of fat to be retained in the liver. If the small droplets flow together to form larger units, they impair the function of the liver cells and the entire metabolism is disturbed.

In the case of non-alcoholic fatty liver, fat droplets also form in the liver, but these cannot be attributed to the degradation substance acetaldehyde. The exact causes are not yet known. However, a combination of various possible underlying diseases, an unfavorable diet and obesity are suspected, which lead to a metabolic disorder. Insulin resistance is related particularly closely to the development of a fatty liver. This is considered a preliminary stage of diabetes and ensures that the body's cells are insensitive to the hormone insulin. The body produces more free fatty acids, which are then transported to the liver because they are not sufficiently broken down. As a result, droplets of fat also form in the liver, which to a certain degree, can restrict the function of the liver cells and thereby burden the liver.

Note: Insulin resistance not only favors fatty liver but fatty liver also the development of insulin resistance and diabetes. The liver cells make fat, and they produce certain proteins, which in turn limit the effectiveness of the body's own insulin. However, the good news here is as soon as the fat deposits in the liver recede, in most cases, the insulin resistance improves at the same time.

If you have been diagnosed with fatty liver, you are not alone. Today, this type of fatty liver is the most common cause of liver disease.

Possible Risk Factors

In addition to insulin resistance, the following causes, among others, are also considered risk factors for the development of fatty liver:

- Diabetes mellitus
- Lipid metabolism disorders
- Obesity
- Malnutrition (especially insufficient intake of protein)

- High sugar consumption
- Increased belly fat
- Sedentary lifestyle
- Autoimmune diseases
- Certain drugs and pollutants
- Genetic factors
- High age

Some doctors today speak of non-alcoholic fatty liver disease as a general metabolic disorder, which in many cases is associated with several diseases such as diabetes, increased obesity or high cholesterol levels. The consequence is not only a restriction in liver function and an increased risk of developing liver inflammation and liver cancer but above all cardiovascular diseases such as high blood pressure, heart attack or stroke. However, especially at the beginning of the diagnosis and a low degree of fatty liver disease, these consequences rarely occur and you can still do a lot to alleviate or even cure the fatty liver by changing your lifestyle.

Symptoms and Diagnosis of Fatty Liver

Many people suffering from fatty liver disease show no symptoms or have severe digestive problems. Generally speaking, the most common symptoms of fatty liver include:

- A sensation of pressure in the right upper abdomen
- Bloating
- Reduced in performance
- Difficulties in concentrating

Only at an advanced stage, it leads to nausea, vomiting, and actual pain in the right upper abdomen. The eyes and skin can also become yellow if the liver function is already significantly altered.

If you have one or more of these symptoms, visit your doctor. They will first investigate your symptoms and perform a preliminary physical examination. Liver enlargement can already be found just by palpating, but the fatty liver can also depend on other causes. So, a laboratory diagnostic determination of the liver values in the blood is generally asked. The latter can show normal range liver values, yet there is a functional impairment of the organ or vice versa. As a consequence, your doctor will make an appointment for an ultrasound with you afterward. In so doing, it can be examined quite well whether and to what extent the fat storage in the liver has already progressed. Whether the stored fats make up more than five percent of the weight of the liver, it is called a fatty liver (the weight of a healthy liver is between 1500 and 2000 grams in an adult). In the case of severe symptoms or unclear findings, your doctor will send you to a specialist who will use a small sample of your liver to examine the condition of the liver cells more precisely.

Exercise

Exercise is a key part of losing weight and maintaining liver health. The meal plans in chapter 3 include specific daily exercise routines in addition to meals. This section discusses the various types of exercises that are important for health.

Cardiovascular Exercise (Cardio)

Cardiovascular exercise, or "cardio," increases the heart rate, improves cardiorespiratory fitness, and reduces fat in the liver. It also helps with maintaining a healthy weight, as well as brain health (with age), healthy skin, and sexual function. Moderate-intensity exercises that will increase heart rate include brisk walking, dancing, tennis, and biking.

Strength Training

Strength training, or resistance exercise, involves activities that improve muscle strength. Some studies have shown that strength training combined with cardiovascular exercise has led to weight loss and a decrease in liver fat. Strength training has also been known to improve fat breakdown and help control sugar levels in the liver. Strength training may be better for some people than cardiovascular exercise because of its lower cardiorespiratory demand, making it more accessible. Moreover, strength training increases muscle mass and more calories being burned at rest. Strength training involves working for different muscle groups with free weights, weighted balls, or weight machines.

Stretching

Flexibility is needed to maintain joint health because it improves joint movement. Lack of flexibility can cause muscle fatigue and place stress on tissues, resulting in muscle injury at other locations besides the site of inflexibility. For example, having very tight calf can induce to knee pain and tendonitis. Stretching for 20 minutes several times a week outside of a training session is beneficial. The benefits of a regular stretching routine include enhanced physical performance, decreased risk of injury, and increased blood supply to joints.

Injury Prevention

Proper precautions must be taken to prevent injury during exercise. The use of appropriate equipment is one component of safe exercise, according to the American Academy of Orthopedic

Surgeons. For example, it's important to replace shoes as they wear out and always wear comfortable clothing. Another consideration is to develop an exercise program that incorporates a variety of types; for example, cardiovascular exercise, strength training, and flexibility.

Stretching is an important component of safe exercise, and it is suggested to hold each stretch for 10 to 20 seconds to be the most effective. Some research has demonstrated that warming up may help in preventing injury as well. Also, be sure to drink enough water to prevent dehydration and remember to keep drinking even during exercise. Having a drink of water every 20 minutes or so can help hydration levels. Adequate rest between training sessions is also an important part of injury prevention.

Environmental Toxins

Environmental toxins are substances that negatively affect health. They also include poisonous chemicals, physical materials and chemical compounds that disrupt biological processes. It's believed that environmental toxins play a role in liver health because evidence of toxin exposure has been seen in geographical areas where many people have liver disease. Particularly, environmental toxins play a major roles in the etiology and progression of NALFD. Exposure to environmental toxins has also been connected with obesity and weight increase. Specific toxin groups to be aware of include the following.

Household Products

Some fragrances, essential oils, paints, polishes, chemicals used in hair products, and other chemicals used in the home have been linked to fatty liver disease. There is still more research needed in this area to understand the full list of toxic chemicals and their lasting impact on the body.

Medications

Different types of medication have been associated with causing liver damage. However, drug-induced liver injury (DILI) occurs in a small number of people exposed to drugs, herbs, or dietary supplements and is not as common as other liver disorders. Some examples of medications that may cause liver damage are vitamin A, nonsteroidal anti-inflammatory drugs (NSAIDs), and glucocorticoids. Drugs may promote the buildup of fat in the liver as well as inflammation and fibrosis. DILI might have severe consequences like life-threatening liver failure, death, or the need for liver transplantation. It is extremely important to follow the dosage amounts when taking medications.

Pesticides

Pesticides are suspected to contribute to NAFLD by negatively impacting fat metabolism. More research is needed in this area because it has been difficult to determine the impact on humans. After all, many studies have been completed on animals. Buying organic foods as much as possible is one way to avoid exposure to pesticides.

Avoiding Toxins in Food

Given the association between pesticides and liver disease, it's important to minimize or avoid exposure. One way to do this is to properly wash produce before cooking or consuming by gently rubbing the food under running water. There is no need to use soap or any other type of wash. For firm produce, use a clean vegetable brush to scrub off any dirt and bacteria. Rinse products before peeling to avoid the transfer of dirt and bacteria from the knife onto the produce. Drying produce with a clean cloth can also help reduce residual bacteria that may be on the surface. Handwashing before and after preparing produce is also important.

A second way to minimize toxins in food is to buy organic foods. Organic versions of many types of foods exist, including produce, grains, and meats. To cut costs, consider buying in bulk or from the freezer section. Using frozen food may be less expensive but it's also a cost-saving because it helps reduce waste. Another way to cut costs is to be on the lookout for slightly blemished or oddly shaped organic produce being sold at a discount.

Sleep

Sleep is important for weight loss. Many studies showed how lack of sleep may have adverse effects. The recommended number of hours to sleep a night is at least seven. Sleeping fewer than seven hours per night regularly is associated with health problems such as obesity, high blood pressure, heart disease, depression, and an increased risk of death. The following steps are a great way to help get better sleep:

Remove electronics one hour before bed. The blue light coming from screens does not help fall asleep as your body thinks is still daytime. A book is an ideal alternative to an electronic device as a way to wind down before bed.

Decrease light exposure close to bedtime. A lot of light in any sleeping environment close to bedtime may make it harder to fall asleep. Consider turning the lights down close to bedtime to prepare for sleep. Try using window shades to make the room darker if there is a lot of light coming from outside.

Get enough physical activity during the day. Being active can help with sleep. It is recommended not to exercise too close to bedtime, however. Leaving enough time between exercise and bedtime allows for body temperature and endorphin levels to return to levels that are conducive to sleep.

Sleep on a consistent schedule. Going to bed and waking up around the same time every day can help maintain a sleep-wake cycle. This means sticking to the schedule and not deviating too much on weekends.

Limit naps during the day. Sleeping too much during the day may make it difficult to fall asleep at night. Limiting the duration of naps to no more than 30 minutes can help.

Stress

Chronic stress has been associated with weight gain, impaired sleep, overeating, and the consumption of foods high in calories, like fat or sugar. To alleviate stress, it's important to move regularly and to take time for self-care. These five steps are a great way to manage stress:

Meditate for 15 minutes a day. Meditation provides an opportunity to slow down, listen, and breathe deeply, all of which are good for both mental and physical health. It may be done silently or through guided meditation.

Regular physical activity. Focusing on the body's movements can help shift away from stressful thoughts or events. Exercise can also help improve sleep, which is an important part of stress management as well. Incorporating cardio, strength training, and flexibility exercises is important when planning to be more active.

Engage with a support network. Having a support network is helpful when it comes to managing life's events. Friends and family may be able to help you take action and move forward. Being ready to navigate a complex situation is important; this might involve gathering resources in advance or bringing in others to help as needed.

Meet with a therapist. Therapists have techniques to assist with self-awareness and how to process unhelpful thoughts. Cognitive behavioral therapy (CBT) is one such approach as it examines the reasons behind certain thoughts and provides alternative ways of looking at situations.

Healthy Habits

Developing healthy habits is important when it comes to weight loss. Getting into a routine of making healthy choices will make it easier to do what is necessary to stay healthy. It is the routine behaviors that will determine health rather than the few instances of eating a certain food. The following behaviors will help form and maintain healthy habits:

Start slow. In the same way that no one would sign up for a marathon without training, jumping into an eating plan cold turkey won't be effective. Make small changes at first and enjoy the food. The same goes for exercise: Walk before running.

Identify food behavior. Notice eating patterns. Be sure to be hungry when eating rather than eating out of boredom or because of stress. Building awareness of eating patterns has an immediate effect and is the best method for making positive changes.

Enjoy food. Pick your favorite foods or add more spice or flavoring to a meal that needs a little help. It's better to enjoy the meal than dread eating it next time. Food should be enjoyed with any diet change, and it's fine to include indulgent foods; just be mindful and conscious of when and how often.

Consistency is key. Dramatic results happen only with a consistent plan. By doing something over and over, a habit will form and those new behaviors will become routine.

Be prepared. Always be ready for those situations where there is little healthy food available. For example, if there is primarily fast food available around the workplace, consider packing a lunch.

Chapter 2. How to Manage Symptoms

The symptoms are going to vary depending on what stage of cirrhosis you are in.

Symptoms at first may be hidden, but as the disease progresses they will present themselves

Here are the most common ones:

- Itchy skin
- Sudden and very rapid weight gain or loss
- Edema presenting with swelling of the legs, ankles and abdomen
- Traces of blood in the stool (even minimal)
- Very persistent fatigue
- Very dark colored urine (orange-brown)
- Little hunger
- Jaundice, which manifests as yellowing of the whites of the eyes or skin.
- Light-colored stools
- Unexplained bruising
- Sudden personality changes including disorientation and confusion.

One of the earliest signs of cirrhosis is edema which is basically the retention of salt and fluid. It often manifests as a slightly swollen leg or ankle at first. With time, the fluid retention extends to your abdomen, a condition known as ascites. When identified early, your doctor will advise you to reduce your intake of salt and also prescribe diuretics. However, if you have a severe case of ascites, your doctor may need to drain the fluid. This is because if the fluid is not drained it could lead to an infected abdomen, referred to as peritonitis.

If left untreated and fluid retention persists to the point that it cannot be treated in any way, a liver transplant may be necessary

How is cirrhosis of the liver managed or treated? Although there is still no complete cure for cirrhosis of the liver, there are treatments that serve to delay its progression and reduce its symptoms, thereby also reducing the damage done to the liver cells.

1. Fluid retention in joints and the abdomen is first managed by following a very low-sodium diet.

   For extreme cases of ascites, the doctor may have to drain the fluid from your stomach.

   Diuretics may also be prescribed to help reduce the fluid buildup.

2. If a patient's cirrhosis is a result of excessive alcohol consumption, then the first step is to refrain from any alcohol intake. This gives the liver a chance to take a break from the detoxification of toxins brought about by alcohol.

3. To improve conditions of mental disorientation and confusion, the best prescription is a healthy low-sodium diet in conjunction with recommended drug therapy. There is a possibility that laxatives may be prescribed to reduce the workload of the liver.

4. In addition to what was mentioned in point three, regular physical activity is highly recommended; in fact, it has been proven to help the body heal

5. In cases of autoimmune hepatitis, the patient will be prescribed drugs that suppress the immune system such as azathioprine.

6. For hemochromatosis patients, treatment will involve removing blood in order lower iron levels thus preventing further liver damage.

7. Do not use non-steroidal anti-inflammatory medication. These include naproxen and ibuprofen. This is because patients with cirrhosis of the liver can further damage their livers and kidneys with such drugs.

8. Individualized treatment of patients with hepatitis C. Individualized treatment of patients with hepatitis C. Not all patients can receive antiviral treatment.. A doctor specializing in liver disease will carry out a series of tests to determine the best course of treatment.

9. Vaccinating patients with cirrhosis against hepatitis A and B infections. This helps prevent further damage to the liver.

Using Diet to Manage Cirrhosis and Chronic Liver Diseases

When the liver is not able to release glycogen, your body starts using its own muscle tissues to provide energy. A situation like this can lead to conditions like malnutrition, weakness and muscle wasting.

If your condition worsens and progresses to cirrhosis, you need to be very careful with your diet. You would need a diet that supports your liver function and also can save you from malnutrition. The best way is to immediately approach a certified doctor or dietician for a strategically designed diet plan.

Let's now talk about various types of cirrhosis conditions and what diet one should eat to keep the liver functioning.

Using Diet to Manage Decompensated Cirrhosis

The second stage of cirrhosis and a dangerous one is called decompensated cirrhosis. This is a condition where the liver is not able to perform all of its normal functions. As a result, a patient may suffer from other severe conditions like fluid retention and mental confusion, known as encephalopathy.

For people suffering from decompensated cirrhosis, a high-energy and high-protein diet is recommended. To be more precise, you would need 35-40kcal and 1.5g of protein for every kg of your body weight per day. It is highly recommended that you must consult your certified doctor for further diet recommendations and treatment.

Handling Fluid Retention

Research shows that in some people with cirrhosis there may be fluid accumulation in the stomach area. Other symptoms of this condition are swelling of the legs and feet. Due to the buildup of fluid in the stomach, one may feel bloated most of the time, but it is highly recommended that the person should drink enough fluids to avoid dehydration.

Cutting down on the amount of common salt in your food can help control fluid retention. The recommendation is to keep the salt content balanced, not too high and not too low. The anticipated amount of salt or sodium reduction in your diet is approximately 5.2 g of salt per day.

The amount of salt in your own prepared food can be controlled but you may not control the salt contents in the foods that are available in the market. It is recommended that you always look at the labels on the food you buy. It will help you keep your salt intake in control.

The best place to look for this information is the nutrition information on the food label. You need to look for the amount of salt per 100g. A portion of food can be called low in salt if the salt content is up to 0.3g salt or less per 100g or 0.1g sodium.

Handling Hepatic Encephalopathy

It has been found in the studies that some people with cirrhosis may develop poor memory and concentration conditions because the damaged liver is not in a position anymore to break the toxins from the bowel which are then supposed to enter the bloodstream and be carried to the brain.

Hepatic encephalopathy can also occur when a person with cirrhosis also has some other conditions such as diarrhea, dehydration, constipation, vomiting and infection or bleeding. In the past, people with hepatic encephalopathy were treated with a low-protein diet but it has now been recognized that this was the wrong approach and that a high-protein diet will help to improve overall liver function. This applies to many internet sites as well that still wrongly suggest that a protein-restricted diet is a solution for this condition.

If you are suffering from hepatic encephalopathy, you should:

- Aim to have 4 to 6 small meals per day that are rich in protein.
- Try to have a snack late in the evening that is high in carbs. This will aid in supporting your liver functions throughout the night.
- Add poultry, eggs, fish and cheese to your diet as these are good alternatives to red meat as a source of protein.
- Add starchy foods such as potatoes, pasta, rice, cereals and pasta to your diet as these foods help in providing energy slowly over a longer period.

Diet to lose weight (Mediterranean)

Mediterranean Diet, when it comes to losing weight, is a popular diet style that has been shown in multiple studies and research to be effective in maintaining a healthy weight while also improving heart health. The Mediterranean Diet is also known as the "Mediterranean-style diet." This diet can help you lose weight, lower blood pressure and cholesterol levels, prevent future disease, protect from cancer or even lower your risk of Alzheimer's disease. There are many different benefits associated with this lifestyle but all can be obtained with very little effort.

The Mediterranean Diet emphasizes the consumption of fresh fruits, vegetables, whole grains and nuts. Instead of focusing on calories, it emphasizes quality. The focus is not on counting intake but rather on eating healthily.

How to Eliminate Toxins from Your Liver for Better Health, Weight Loss, and Energy

As we have stated throughout the previous chapters, the liver is responsible for metabolizing fats, which, unlike proteins and carbs, are very difficult to digest. It's therefore prudent to avoid excessive consumption of fats to avoid overworking your liver which can lead to fatty liver disease, as is the case with people suffering from obesity.

- **Caution when taking medication:**

Sometimes, combining medications can heavily tax your liver. So, it's always advisable that all medications you use to be prescribed by a medical professional. Moreover, do not mix medications with natural remedies since this can also overwhelm your liver. Avoid mixing alcohol with medicine, as this can be too heavy on your liver to the point of liver failure. You must ask your doctor if it's okay to drink alcohol with your prescribed medications.

- **Avoid excessive consumption of alcohol:**

Heavy alcohol consumption causes cirrhosis of the liver over time. The process of your liver breaking down alcohol involves the production of free radicals and chemicals such as acetaldehyde. To seriously damage your liver, it takes approximately a liter of wine, or its equivalent daily for 20 years in the case of women. For women, it takes less than half.

- **Practice safe sex:**

Currently, there is no vaccination to prevent hepatitis C. Consequently, you should behave cautiously for sex, piercings, and tattoos.

- **Avoid aerosol/ airborne chemicals:**

If you decide to use gardening, housecleaning chemicals, and paint, ensure that your environment is well-ventilated and put on a mask. Try as much as possible to limit your inhalation of toxins since the liver must process all toxins, which can lead to liver problems, especially if you are regularly exposed to toxic agents.

- **Get the necessary vaccinations:**

You must get vaccinated, especially if you plan to travel where malaria, Hepatitis A and B may be aconcern. Yellow fever causes liver failure, and malaria grows and multiplies in your liver. Take the necessary precautions by having the recommended vaccines and drugs.

- **Avoid exposure to foreign blood and germs:**

If you come in contact with another person's blood, you should visit your doctor for immediate medical attention. Also, avoid sharing personal items such as needles and toothbrushes. Avoid exposing yourself to toxins.

Natural Remedies (Herbs and Ayurvedic Remedies)

The good news is that natural remedies for fatty liver disease exist! Herbs and Ayurvedic remedies are two types of treatments that may help improve symptoms and even reverse the effects of this common condition.

How do Ayurvedic Remedies for Fatty Liver Disease Work? By restoring the balance in a person's overall body system, Ayurvedic therapy heals many health conditions including fatty liver disease. This therapy focuses on the body's essential energy that is stored in the blood, known as "prana." With a healthy, balanced system of prana circulating freely through the body, a person can achieve good health. Some Ayurvedic remedies have also been found to help with fatty liver disease.

Herbal and Other Fatty Liver Remedies

Although simple nonalcoholic fatty liver disease is a relatively new discovery, people have known since ancient times that the liver can become diseased. Because medical science as we know it today did not exist in these early times, healing practitioners turned to herbal remedies. And luckily for you, if you have fatty liver disease, they still work beautifully.

Herbs to Use for Fatty Liver

Throughout history, many specific herbs have been identified as having the properties to help with liver disorders. Remember that a little of most herbs goes a long way. Herbs are natural, but they can also be very potent. This is an important fact if you need to take medications for a significant health problem. An essential rule of thumb is to consult with your doctor if you have any questions about using herbs in conjunction with medications. Here is a list of some of the herbs that have been used to help with fatty liver.

Milk Thistle

Milk thistle is perhaps the most scientifically studied herb for the treatment of liver disorders. It has consistently been shown to help with fatty liver in many research studies. Milk thistle was first noticed in the Mediterranean area, but for the intervening millennia, it has spread throughout the world. Its primary medicinal ingredient is silymarin. You can find milk thistle products in capsule, liquid extract and tincture forms. They are generally standardized to contain 70% to 80% silymarin extracted from the milk thistle seeds.

Dandelion Root

Did you know that many bitter foods are actually healthful for the liver? A prime example is the dandelion root. This herb is considered by most people to be a weed, and it is very commonly found in most places around the world. It is often included in liver tonic powders, liquids and capsules. Dandelion root is beneficial for reducing symptoms of fatty liver problems, including:

- Fatigue
- Headaches
- Sugar cravings
- Bad breath
- Irritability
- Abdominal swelling
- Skin problems
- Excess weight

Comfrey

Be careful not to use too much comfrey. The safest part of the comfrey plant is the root. However, the FDA has warned that comfrey can cause serious medical problems including liver damage. So, if you use this herb, use it sparingly, and use only the root.

Wild Yam Root

Wild yam root, in addition to its benefits for reproductive health, can help with bile production, which is important to good liver health. Having proper bile production decreases congestion in the liver and prevents bile stones; this should not be used during the pregnancy stage or while breastfeeding. You also need to avoid wild yam root if you have a hormone-related health problem such as breast cancer, ovarian cancer and the like.

Licorice Root

The main studies on licorice root have focused on treatment for chronic hepatitis C and liver cancer. However, herbalists have long used this root for less serious liver disorders, most recently for fatty liver. There are usually no side effects in any case, so it is a reasonably safe herb to try for fatty liver.

Liverwort

Liverwort is one of the most used herbal treatments for liver ailments. The recommended dosage is 3.8 grams, which amounts to about 4 teaspoons (1 tablespoon) of the commercial liquid extract of liverwort. As long as you keep checking this dosage, you do not have to worry about side effects or toxicity. If you want a more exact dosage, premeasured capsules are now available.

Burdock

Little research has been done on the burdock plant as a treatment for liver disorders. However, it has been used for many ages as a blood-cleanser. It also has lots of Vitamin E and B Vitamins that can help repair your liver or even prevent damage to your liver.

Special Herbal Tea for Fatty Liver

One traditional remedy for liver disease was a tea made of a special combination of herbs. In his book titled "The Amazing Liver and Gallbladder Flush," Andreas Moritz gives a recipe for a similar tea. What you need to do is to combine the herbs with water in a pot and let them soak overnight. Then, pour off the water and heat to make your tea. Here's the recipe:

Combine:

- 1 part Dandelion root
- ½ part Comfrey root
- 1 part Licorice root
- 1 part Agrimony
- 1 part Wild yam root
- 1 part Barberry bark
- 1 part Bearsfoot
- 1 part Tanners oak bark
- 1 part Milk thistle herb

Special Herbal Tea for Gallstones

Moritz also suggests that the problem of fatty liver is caused by the formation of gallstones that crowd and block off structures in the liver. To prevent these gallstones from forming and to help release them from the liver, Moritz suggests regularly drinking the following mixture:

- Uva Ursi
- Marjoram
- Comfrey root
- Fennel seed
- Marshmallow root
- Chicory herb
- Hydrangea root

- Cat's claw
- Gravel root
- Golden rod herb

Another tea that can reduce liver problems is made from the bark of the lapacho tree. You might find this natural remedy under the names of Pau d'Arco, Ipe Roxo or Taheebo. Native Americans have long used the herb chaparral to treat liver disease as well.

Other Natural Remedies

Drink Hot Ionized Water

Hot, ionized water is helpful for liver dysfunction because of the charge of its electrons. Its negative ions neutralize and carry off toxic positive ions from your body tissues. To make ionized water, simply boil some water for 15 minutes. Keep it in a closed container and sip from it frequently throughout the day.

Drink Enough Water

Drink plenty of clean, pure water – about 6 to 8 glasses of water. Make sure to drink a glass of water when you first get up and after each meal. Without enough water, you not only become dehydrated; you also limit the amount of water available for the production of bile that is needed for proper digestion.

Oil Therapy

Oil therapy is an easy way to clear toxins from your upper digestive tract. Start with one tablespoon of cold-pressed, unrefined oil such as sunflower, olive or sesame oil. Swish it in your mouth for some minutes, moving it over and under your tongue and between your teeth. Then, spit the oil out and rinse your mouth. For the rinse, you can stir either one-half teaspoon of sea salt or one-half teaspoon of baking soda into the water until it is dissolved. After you rinse, brush your teeth to remove any oily residue.

Chapter 3. How to Manage Fatty Liver with Diet

To combat fatty liver disease, you must make long-term changes to your diet rather than simply avoiding or incorporating random foods here and there. "The most important aspect of these changes is that they are long-term," says Aymin Delgado-Borrego, MD, a pediatric and young adult gastroenterologist and public health specialist at Kidz Medical Services in Florida. In general, the best diet for fatty liver includes the following foods:

- Adequate fiber

- Lots of fruits, vegetables, and nuts

- Whole grains

- Very limited saturated fats from animal products

- Very limited salt and sugar

- No alcohol

The American Liver Foundation suggests cutting back on calories and modeling you're eating habits after the Mediterranean diet. According to Dr. Delgado-Borrego, half of any plate of food should be fruits and vegetables, one-quarter of protein, and the other quarter of starches. You can always refer to the foods to eat and avoid, or simply remember these two main rules for fatty liver improvement:

1. Choose low-calorie, Mediterranean-style foods. Consume plenty of plant-based foods, whole grains, extra virgin olive oil, and fish, while limiting your intake of poultry, cheese, and other dairy products.
2. Avoid refined grains, processed meats, and added sugars.

"The best way to ensure significant resolution or even cure [fatty liver disease] is to lose approximately 7%-10% of your body weight," says Austin Gastroenterology's Sanaa Arastu, MD.

8 Foods to Eat

Experts recommend these foods in particular for a healthy liver:

1. Almond milk or low-fat cow's milk: Adults and children with fatty liver disease, according to Dr. Delgado-Borrego, should consume calcium with caution. "Over the last couple of years, there has been some emerging evidence that adequate calcium and vitamin D intake may help to prevent the development of fatty liver disease," she explains, adding that more research is needed. "In addition, patients with advanced liver disease may develop early osteopenia and

osteoporosis due to multiple nutritional complications." Fatty liver disease does not always impair calcium absorption. Calcium is simply essential for everyone." Drink up to three glasses of either of these kinds of milk per day.

2. Coffee: Coffee, without added sugar or creamers, is one of the most effective ways to improve fatty liver at the moment. "It appears that coffee may reduce gut permeability, making it more difficult for people to absorb fats," Dr. Delgado-Borrego explains. "However, this is still being investigated, and the answer to this question is not yet entirely clear." Nonetheless, there is mounting evidence that coffee can aid in the prevention of fatty liver disease." Multiple cups of coffee might be recommended, depending on the patient.

3. Foods are high in vitamin E, such as red bell peppers, spinach, peanuts, and nuts: Dr. Delgado-Borrego recommends these vitamin E-rich foods to people with fatty liver. While more research is needed, one study concluded that the vitamin helps people with NAFLD or NASH in a minor way.

4. Water: Experts recommend drinking half an ounce to one ounce of water per pound of body weight per day to avoid dehydration and adverse effects on the liver.

5. Olive oil: Olive oil and avocado oil, for example, can provide healthy fats. These help with satiety and lower liver enzyme levels. Other monounsaturated fat-rich oils include sesame, peanut, sunflower, canola, and safflower oil.

6. Flax and chia seeds: These are plant sources of omega-3 acids. Dietitian Sandy Younan Brikho, MDA, RDN, recommends these seeds for overall liver health as they help reduce fat levels in the organ.

7. Garlic: One study suggests that eating more garlic over a 15-week period led to a decrease in body fat mass in people with NAFLD, consequently also decreasing fat in the liver.

8. Soy: Some research states that consuming soy products brings improvements in metabolic effect in people with NAFLD.

8 Foods to Avoid

Foods to avoid include those that cause blood sugar spikes or weight gain, such as:

1. Fruit juices, sodas and sugary drinks are all enemies of the liver.
2. Low-calorie diet drinks: these are sugar substitutes that cause more liver damage
3. Butter and ghee: these foods are high in saturated fat, which is why they are absolutely not good for the liver
4. Baked goods and sweet desserts: Absolutely to avoid if you want to get well
5. Bacon, sausage, cured meats, and fatty meats: These are high in saturated fats, and therefore not recommended by our experts.

6. Alcohol: Our experts advise against doing this if you have fatty liver disease caused by excessive drinking, as it will simply cause more liver damage. It is acceptable for those with NAFLD to consume alcohol on occasion, such as a glass of wine.
7. Salty foods: Some research has suggested that NAFLD is worsened by salt consumption, most often because salt-rich foods are also the most caloric and fatty foods
8. Fried foods: Fried foods also have too many calories and have no place in any healthy diet

Shopping list for a meal plan

Many of the items listed below are considered pantry staples and will last for several weeks or even months, for example, spices, seeds, and dry baking ingredients. These items will not need to be replaced every week. Always buy produce that is organic and fresh, rather than packaged, where possible.

Produce:

- Organic spinach – 2 bags
- Romaine lettuce head
- Asparagus – 1 lb
- Carrots – 2 bunches
- Red or yellow peppers – 2
- Celery – 1 bunch
- Grape tomatoes – 1 container
- Red onion – 1
- Green onions – 1 bunch
- Zucchini – 2–3
- Sweet potatoes – 2
- Green Beans – ½ lb
- Avocados – 4
- Cucumbers – 2 or 3
- Fresh cilantro – 1 bunch
- Organic berries of choice
- Limes – 2
- Lemons – 6
- Fresh ginger
- Frozen strawberries

Poultry, Seafood, Meat, Eggs, and Dairy:

- Pastured organic eggs – 2–3 dozen
- Pre-cooked rotisserie chicken – 1 OR Boneless, skinless chicken breasts – 2 lb
- Wild salmon fillet – 2 lb
- Cod – 1 lb
- Sweet Italian chicken sausage – 1 ½ lb
- Flank steak – 2 lb
- Organic ground beef, bison, or turkey – 1 lb
- Water-packed tuna – 2 cans
- Nitrite and nitrate-free lunch meat – 1 package
- Organic, low-fat, plain Greek yogurt – 16 oz
- Coconut milk
- Protein: in Common Items

Nuts, Seeds, Oils, Flours, and Spices:

- Raw pumpkin seeds
- Raw cashews
- Raw almonds
- Raw walnuts
- Almond butter – 1 jar
- Almond flour
- Chia seeds
- Poppy seeds
- Vanilla extract
- Fresh honey (preferably local)
- Cold-pressed coconut oil
- Favorite seasonings: garlic salt, paprika, etc.
- Baking soda

Miscellaneous:

- Jarred, roasted red peppers (water-packed)
- Favorite fresh salsa
- Hummus
- Raw, unfiltered apple cider vinegar
- Vanilla protein powder

Chapter 4. Breakfast Recipes

1. Farro Salad

Preparation Time: 10 minutes

Cooking Time: 4 minutes

Servings: 2

Ingredients:

- 1 tbsp olive oil
- A pinch salt and black pepper
- 1 bunch baby spinach, chopped
- 1 avocado, pitted, peeled, and chopped
- 1 garlic clove, minced
- 2 cups farro, already cooked
- ½ cup cherry tomatoes, cubed

Directions

Heat a pan with oil over medium heat. Add spinach and all the other ingredients, then toss and cook for 4 minutes.

When ready, divide into bowls and serve.

Nutrition

Calories: 361, Fat: 28.5 g Fiber: 2.7 g Carbs: 28.3 g Protein: 2.8 g

2. Chili Avocado Scramble

Preparation Time: 10 minutes

Cooking Time: 10 minutes

Servings: 4

Ingredients:
- 4 eggs, beaten
- 1 white onion, diced
- 1 tbsp avocado oil
- 1 avocado, finely chopped
- ½ tsp chili flakes
- 1 oz Cheddar cheese, shredded
- ½ tsp salt
- 1 tbsp fresh parsley

Directions

Pour the avocado oil into the pan and bring it to a boil.

Then add diced onion and roast it until it is light brown.

Meanwhile, mix up together chili flakes, beaten eggs, and salt.

Pour the resulting mixture over the cooked onion and cook the mixture for about 1.5 minutes over medium-low heat.

After this, scramble the eggs well with the help of a fork or spatula. Cook the eggs until they are solid but soft.

After this, add chopped avocado and shredded cheese.

Stir the scramble well and transfer it to the serving plates.
1.   Sprinkle the meal with fresh parsley.

Calories: 235, Fat: 20.1 g Fiber: 4 g Carbs: 7.4 g Protein: 8.6 g

3. Tapioca Pudding

Preparation Time: 10 minutes

Cooking Time: 15 minutes

Servings: 3

Ingredients:

- ¼ cup pearl tapioca
- ¼ cup maple syrup
- 2 cups almond milk
- ½ cup coconut flesh, shredded
- 1 ½ tsp lemon juice

Directions

- In a pan, combine the milk with the tapioca and the rest of the ingredients, bring to a simmer over medium heat, and cook for 15 minutes.

- Divide the mix into bowls, cool it down and serve for breakfast.

Calories: 361, Fat: 28.5 g Fiber: 2.7 g Carbs: 28.3 g Protein: 2.8 g

4. Cauliflower Hash Brown Breakfast Bowl

Preparation Time: 10 minutes

Cooking Time: 30 minutes

Servings: 2

Ingredients:
- 1 tbsp lemon juice
- 1 egg & 1 avocado
- 1 tsp garlic powder
- 2 tbsp extra virgin olive oil
- 2 oz mushrooms, sliced
- ½ green onion, chopped
- ¼ cup salsa
- ¾ cup cauliflower rice
- ½ small handful baby spinach

Directions

Using a small bowl Mash together avocado, lemon juice, garlic powder, salt and black pepper in a small bowl.

Take another bowl and Whisk eggs, salt and black pepper in a bowl and keep aside.

Heat half of the olive oil over medium heat using a skillet and add mushrooms.

Sauté for about 3 minutes and season with garlic powder, salt, and pepper.

Sauté again for another 2 minutes approximately and dish out in a bowl.

- Add the rest of the olive oil and add cauliflower, garlic powder, salt and pepper.
- Sauté for almost 5 minutes and dish out.
- Put the mushrooms in the skillet again, then add green onions and baby spinach.
- Sauté for about 30 seconds and add whisked eggs.
- Cook for approximately 1 minute and pour on the sautéed cauliflower hash browns.
- Top using salsa and mashed avocado, then serve.

Nutrition

Nutrition: Calories: 400, Carbs: 15.8 g Fat: 36.7 g Protein: 8 g Sodium: 288 mg Sugar: 4.2 g

5. Pumpkin Coconut Oatmeal Bowl

Preparation Time: 10 minutes

Cooking Time: 13 minutes

Servings: 6

Ingredients:

- 2 cups oatmeal
- 1 cup coconut milk
- 1 cup milk
- 1 tsp pumpkin pie spices
- 2 tbsp pumpkin puree
- 1 tbsp honey
- ½ small handful baby spinach
- Salt and black pepper, to taste

Directions

- Pour coconut milk and milk into the saucepan. Bring the liquid to boil.
- Add oatmeal, mix well with a spoon. .
- Simmer oatmeal for 8 minutes over medium-low heat.
- Meanwhile, stir together honey, cake spices and pumpkin puree.
- When the oatmeal is cooked, add the pumpkin puree mixture and stir for a few minutes.
- Place on serving plates.

Nutrition

Nutrition: Calories: 232 Fat: 12.5 g Fiber: 3.8 g Carbs: 26.2 g Protein: 5.9 g

6. Toasted Crostini

Preparation Time: 10 minutes

Cooking Time: 15 minutes

Servings: 4

Ingredients:

- 12 slices (⅓-inch thick) whole-wheat baguette, toasted
- Coarse salt and freshly ground pepper

For the spread:

- 1 can chickpeas (15 ½ oz), drained, rinsed
- ¼ cup olive oil, extra-virgin
- 1 tbsp lemon juice, freshly squeezed
- 1 small clove garlic, minced
- 2 tbsp olive oil, extra-virgin, divided
- 2 tbsp celery, finely diced, plus celery leaves for garnish
- 8 large green olives, pitted, cut into ⅛-inch slivers

Directions

Using a food processor, combine the spread ingredients and season with salt and pepper. Then, set the mixture aside.

Put together 1 tablespoon of olive oil and the remaining ingredients in a small mixing bowl. Season with salt and pepper and set aside.

Divide the spread over the toasted baguette slices, and top using the relish. Drizzle the remaining 1 tablespoon of olive oil over each slice and season with pepper. If you like, garnish using celery leaves. Serve immediately

Nutrition

Nutrition: Calories: 603, Total Fat: 3.7 g Sat. Fat: 3.7 g Cholesterol: 0 mg Sodium: 781 mg Pot: 483 mg Carbs: 79.2 g Fiber: 9.6 g Sugar: 6.8 g Protein: 19.1 g

7. Heavenly Egg Bake with Blackberry

Preparation Time: 10 minutes

Cooking Time: 15 minutes

Servings: 4

Ingredients:

- Chopped rosemary
- 1 tsp lime zest
- ½ tsp salt
- ¼ tsp vanilla extract, unsweetened
- 1 tsp grated ginger
- 3 tbsp coconut flour
- 5 organic eggs
- 1 tbsp olive oil
- ½ cup fresh blackberries
- Black pepper to taste

Directions

Preheat the oven to 350°F.

In the mean time, put all the ingredients in a blender, except for the berries, and pulse for 2 to 3 minutes until the mixture is well blended and smooth.

Take 4 silicon muffin cups and grease them with oil. Then, evenly distribute the blendedbatter in the cups and top using black pepper. Cook them in the oven for 15 minutes until the top has golden brown.

When done, let blueberry eggs bake cool in the muffin cups for 5 minutes, then take them out, cool them on a wire rack and then serve.

In case of meal preparation, wrap each egg bakes using aluminum foil and freeze for up to 3days.

When you want to eat them, reheat blueberry egg bakes using the microwave and serve.

Nutrition

Calories: 144, Fat: 10 g Carbs: 2 g Protein: 8.5 g

8. Quick Cream of Wheat

Preparation Time: 10 minutes

Cooking Time: 12 minutes

Servings: 1

Ingredients:
- 4 cups whole milk
- ½ cup farina
- ½ tsp salt
- 3 tbsp sugar
- 3 tbsp pine nuts

Directions

In a large saucepan over medium heat, bring whole milk to a simmer, and cook for about 4 minutes. Do not allow milk to scorch.

Whisk in farina, salt, and sugar, and bring to a slight boil. Cook for 2 minutes, reduce heat to low and cook for 3 more minutes. Stay close to the pan to ensure it doesn't boil over.

Pour mixture into 4 bowls, and let cool for 5 minutes.

Meanwhile, in a small pan over low heat, cook pine nuts for about 3 minutes or until pine nuts are lightly toasted.

Evenly spoon pine nuts over each bowl, and

Nutrition

Nutrition: Calories: 165, Carbs: 3 g Fat: 10 g Protein: 12 g

9. Feta and Eggs Mix

Preparation Time: 10 minutes

Cooking Time: 5 minutes

Servings: 4

Ingredients:
- 4 eggs, beaten
- ½ tsp ground black pepper
- 2 oz Feta, scrambled
- ½ tsp salt
- 1 tsp fresh parsley, chopped

Directions

Add beaten eggs to a skillet

Then add parsley, salt, and scrambled eggs. Cook the eggs for 1 minute over high heat.

Add ground black pepper and scramble eggs with the help of the fork.

Cook the eggs for 3 minutes over medium-high heat.

Nutrition

Nutrition: Calories: 110 Fat: 8.4 g Fiber: 0.1 g Carbs: 1.1 g Protein: 7.6 g

10. Banana Pancakes

Preparation Time: 10 minutes

Cooking Time: 20 minutes

Servings: 4

Ingredients:
- 1 cup whole wheat flour
- ¼ tsp baking soda
- ¼ tsp baking powder
- 1 cup mashed banana
- 2 eggs
- 1 cup milk

Directions

In a bowl combine all ingredients and mix well.

In a skillet heat olive oil.

Pour ¼ of the batter and cook each pancake for 1-2 minutes per side.

When ready remove from heat and serve.

Nutrition

Nutrition: Calories: 210, Carbs: 7 g Fat: 14 g Protein: 15 g

11. Nectarine Pancakes

Preparation Time: 10 minutes

Cooking Time: 30 minutes

Servings: 4

Ingredients:
- 1 cup whole wheat flour
- ¼ tsp baking soda
- ¼ tsp baking powder
- 1 cup nectarines
- 2 eggs
- 1 cup milk

Directions

In a bowl combine all ingredients and mix well.

In a skillet heat olive oil.

Pour ¼ of the batter and cook each pancake for 1-2 minutes per side.

When ready remove from heat and serve.

Nutrition

Nutrition: Calories: 210, Carbs: 7 g Fat: 14 g Protein: 15 g

12. Raspberry Pudding

Preparation Time: 10 minutes

Cooking Time: 30 minutes

Servings: 2

Ingredients:
- ½ cup raspberries
- 2 tsp maple syrup
- 1 ½ cup Plain yogurt
- ¼ tsp ground cardamom
- ⅓ cup Chia seeds, dried

Directions

Mix up together Plain yogurt with maple syrup and ground cardamom.

Add Chia seeds. Stir it gently.

Put the yogurt in the serving glasses and top with the raspberries.

Refrigerate the breakfast for at least 30 minutes or overnight.

Nutrition

Nutrition: Calories: 305, Fat: 11.5 g Fiber: 11.8 g Carbs: 33.2 g Protein: 15.5 g

13. Detox Porridge

Preparation Time: 10 minutes

Cooking Time: 2 minutes

Servings: 2

Ingredients:
- 1 cup unsweetened almond milk
- 2 tbsp ground golden flax
- ½ cup coconut flour
- 1 tbsp coconut oil
- 1 tsp cinnamon
- 1 cup water
- 1 tbsp raw honey
- Toasted coconut to serve
- Toasted almonds to serve

Directions

Using a microwave-safe bowl, stir together all the ingredients until well mixed; put it in themicrowave and heat for 1 minute.

Stir again to combine well and microwave for another 1 minute. Serve immediately topped with toasted almonds and toasted coconut.

Nutrition: Calories: 303, Fat: 11.2 g Fiber: 11.8 g Carbs: 33.2 g Protein: 15.5 g

14. Avocado Crab Omelet

Preparation Time: 10 minutes

Cooking Time: 10 minutes

Servings: 2

Ingredients:
- ¼ lb crab meat
- 4 large free-range eggs, beaten
- ½ medium avocado, diced
- 1 medium tomato, diced
- 1 tsp olive oil
- ⅛ tsp freshly ground black pepper
- A pinch salt
- 1 tbsp freshly chopped cilantro

Directions

Cook crab in a skillet according to the instructions on the packet. Then, chop the cooked crab and set it aside.

Using a small bowl, toss together avocado, tomato, and cilantro; season with sea salt and pepper and set aside.

Take a separate bowl, beat the eggs, and set aside.

Set a skillet over medium heat, then add olive oil and heat until hot.

Put half of the egg in the skillet and tilt the skillet until covering the bottom. When almostcooked, add crab onto one side of the egg and fold it in half. Cook for another minute and top using the avocado-tomato mixture.

For the second omelet, repeat with the remaining ingredients.

Nutrition

Nutrition: Calories: 242, Carbs: 7 g Fat: 19 g Protein: 12 g

15. Buckwheat Pancakes

Preparation Time: 10 minutes

Cooking Time: 15 minutes

Servings: 3

Ingredients:
- ½ cup buckwheat flour
- 2 ripe bananas
- 2 tbsp olive
- 2 tbsp water
- 1 tsp ground cinnamon
- 1 tsp vanilla extract
- ½ tsp baking soda
- 2 tsp apple cider vinegar
- ¼ cup fresh blueberries for serving

Directions

Preheat your oven to 350°F.

Add the ripe banana to a large bowl and mash until smooth; whisk in ground buckwheat flour, water, oil, vanilla, vinegar, cinnamon, and baking powder until well combined.

Heat a skillet over medium heat; add in oil and heat until hot but not smoky; add in about a quarter cup of batter and spread to cover the bottom of the pan.

Cook for about 2 minutes and then flip to cook the other side for about 1 minute or until browned.

Serve right away topped with fresh blueberries.

Nutrition

Nutrition: Calories: 242, Carbs: 7 g Fat: 19 g Protein: 12 g

16. Apple Oatmeal

Preparation Time: 10 minutes

Cooking Time: 8 minutes

Servings: 3

Ingredients:
- ½ tsp ground cinnamon
- 4 tbsp fat-free vanilla yogurt
- 1 ½ cup quick oats
- ¼ cup maple syrup
- 3 cups apple juice
- ¼ cup raisins
- ½ cup chopped apple
- ¼ cup chopped walnuts

Directions

Put cinnamon and apple juice in a saucepan and make them boil.

Add raisins, maple syrup, apples, and oats.

Switch the heat to low and cook while stirring until most of the juice is absorbed. Fold in walnuts and serve, topped with yogurt.

Nutrition

Nutrition: Calories: 242, Carbs: 25 g Fat: 12 g Protein: 13 g

17. Raspberry Overnight Porridge

Preparation Time: Overnight

Cooking Time: 0 Minute

Servings: 12

Ingredients:
- ⅓ cup rolled oats
- ½ cup almond milk
- 1 tbsp honey
- 5-6 raspberries, fresh or canned and unsweetened

Directions

Add oats, almond milk, and honey in a mason jar and put it into the fridge overnight.

Serve the following morning, topped with raspberries.

Nutrition

Nutrition: Calories: 143.6, Carbs: 34.62 g Protein: 3.44 g Sodium: 77.88 mg Potassium: 153.25 mg Phosphorus: 99.3 mg Dietary Fiber: 7.56 g Fat: 3.91 g

18. Cheesy Scrambled Eggs with Fresh Herbs

Preparation Time: 15 minutes

Cooking Time: 10 minutes

Servings: 4

Ingredients:
- 3 eggs
- 2 egg whites
- ½ cup cream cheese
- ¼ cup unsweetened rice milk
- 1 tbsp green part only chopped scallion
- 1 tbsp chopped fresh tarragon
- ground black pepper to taste

Directions

In a container, combine eggs, egg whites, cream cheese, rice milk, scallions, and tarragon until mixed and smooth.

Pour in the egg mix and cook, stirring, for 5 minutes or until the eggs are thick and curds creamy.

Season using pepper, then serve.

Nutrition

Nutrition: Calories: 220 Fat: 19.2 g Carbs: 3.1 g Phosphorus: 220 mg Potassium: 141 mg Sodium: 195 mg Protein: 7 g

19. Turkey and Spinach Scramble on Melba Toast

Preparation Time: 2 minutes

Cooking Time: 15 minutes

Servings: 2

Ingredients:
- 1 tsp extra virgin olive oil
- 1 cup raw spinach
- ½ clove, minced garlic
- 1 tsp grated nutmeg
- 1 cup cooked and diced turkey breast
- 4 slices melba toast
- 1 tsp balsamic vinegar

Directions

Heat a pot over a source of heat and add oil.

Add turkey and heat for almost 6 or 8 minutes.

Add spinach, garlic, and nutmeg and stir-fry for another 6 minutes.

Plate up the Melba toast, topped with spinach and turkey scramble

Drizzle using balsamic vinegar, then serve.

Nutrition: Calories: 301 Fat: 19 g Carbs: 12 g Phosphorus: 215 mg Potassium: 269 mg Sodium: 360 mg Protein: 19 g

20. Vegetable Omelet

Preparation Time: 15 minutes

Cooking Time: 10 minutes

Servings: 3

Ingredients:
- 4 egg whites
- 1 egg
- 2 tablespoons chopped fresh parsley
- 2 tablespoons water
- olive oil spray
- ½ cup chopped and boiled red bell pepper
- ¼ cup, both green and white parts chopped scallion

Directions

Whisk together the egg, egg whites, parsley, and water until well blended. Set aside.

Spray a skillet with olive oil spray and place over medium heat.

Sauté the peppers and scallion for 3 minutes or until softened.

Over the vegetables, you can now pour the egg and cook, swirling the skillet, for 2 minutes or until the edges start to set. Cook until set.

Season with black pepper and serve.

Nutrition: Calories: 75 Fat: 3.1 g Carbs: 2.1 g Phosphorus: 68 mg Potassium: 195 mg Sodium: 230 mg Protein: 11 g 20

21. Walnuts Yogurt Mix

Preparation Time: 10 minutes

Cooking Time: 0 minutes

Servings: 6

Ingredients

- 2 ½ cups Greek yogurt
- 1 ½ cup walnuts, chopped
- 1 tsp vanilla extract
- ¾ cup honey
- 2 tsp cinnamon powder

Directions

In a bowl, combine the yogurt with the walnuts and the rest of the ingredients, toss, divide into smaller bowls and keep in the fridge for 10 minutes before serving for breakfast.

Nutrition

Nutrition: Calories: 388 g Fat: 24.6 g Fiber: 2.9 g Carbs: 39.1 g Protein: 10.2 g

22. Mediterranean Egg-feta Scramble

Preparation Time: 10 minutes

Cooking Time: 20 minutes

Servings: 4

Ingredients:

- 6 eggs
- ¾ cup crumbled feta cheese
- 2 tbsp green onions, minced
- 2 tbsp red peppers, roasted, diced
- ¼ tsp kosher salt
- ¼ tsp garlic powder
- ¼ cup Greek yogurt
- ½ tsp dry oregano
- ½ tsp dry basil
- 1 tsp olive oil
- A few cracks freshly ground black pepper
- Warm whole-wheat tortillas, optional

Directions

Preheat a skillet over medium heat.

In a bowl, whisk the eggs, sour cream, basil, oregano, garlic powder, salt, and pepper. Gently add the feta.

When the skillet is hot, add the olive oil and then the egg mixture; allow the egg mix to set then scrape the bottom of the pan to let the uncooked egg cook. Stir in the red peppers and the green onions. Continue cooking until the egg mixture is cooked to your preferred doneness. Serve immediately.

If desired, sprinkle with extra feta and then wrap the scrambled eggs in tortillas.

Nutrition

Nutrition: Calories: 260 Total Fat: 16 g Sat. Fat: 8 g Cholesterol: 350 mg Sodium: 750 mg Pot: 190 mg Carbs: 12 g Fiber: >1 g Sugar: 2 g Protein: 16 g

23. Spiced Chickpeas Bowls

Preparation Time: 10 minutes

Cooking Time: 30 minutes

Servings: 4

Ingredients:

- 15 oz canned chickpeas, drained and rinsed
- ¼ tsp cardamom, ground
- ½ tsp cinnamon powder
- 1 ½ tsp turmeric powder
- 1 tsp coriander, ground
- 1 tbsp olive oil
- A pinch salt and black pepper
- ¾ cup Greek yogurt
- ½ cup green olives, pitted and halved
- ½ cup cherry tomatoes, halved
- 1 cucumber, sliced

Directions

Spread the chickpeas on a lined baking sheet, add cardamom, cinnamon, turmeric, coriander, oil, a pinch of salt and pepper, stir, and bake at 370°F for about 35 minutes

Take a bowl and combine the roasted chickpeas with the rest of the ingredients, now mix everything together and serve for breakfast.

Nutrition: Calories: 519 Fat: 34.5 g Fiber: 13.3 g Carbs: 49.8 g Protein: 12 g

24. Orzo and Veggie Bowls

Preparation Time: 10 minutes

Cooking Time: 0 minutes

Servings: 4

Ingredients:
- 2 ½ cups whole-wheat orzo, cooked
- 14 oz canned cannellini beans, drained and rinsed
- 1 yellow bell pepper, cubed
- 1 green bell pepper, cubed
- A pinch salt and black pepper
- 3 tomatoes, cubed
- 1 red onion, chopped
- 1 cup mint, chopped
- 2 cups feta cheese, crumbled
- 2 tbsp olive oil
- ¼ cup lemon juice
- 1 tbsp lemon zest, grated
- 1 cucumber, cubed
- 1 ¼ cup kalamata olives, pitted and sliced
- 3 garlic cloves, minced

Directions

In a salad bowl, combine the barley with the beans, peppers and the rest of the ingredients, then mix everything and finally divide the mixture among plates and serve for breakfast.

Nutrition: Calories: 411 Fat: 17 g Fiber: 13 g Carbs: 51 g Protein: 14 g

25. Vanilla Oats

Preparation Time: 10 minutes

Cooking Time: 10 minutes

Servings: 4

Ingredients:
- ½ cup rolled oats
- 1 cup milk
- 1 tsp vanilla extract
- 1 tsp ground cinnamon
- 2 tsp honey
- 2 tbsp Plain yogurt

Directions

Put milk into the saucepan and bring it to boil.

Add rolled oats and stir well.

Close the lid and simmer the oats for 5 minutes over medium heat until the oats will absorb all milk

Whisk together plain yogurt with honey, cinnamon, and vanilla extract using separate serving bowls.

Put the cooked oats into the serving bowls.

Top the oats using the yogurt mixture in the shape of the wheel.

Nutrition

Nutrition: Calories: 243 Fat: 20.2 g Fiber: 1 g Carbs: 2.8 g Protein: 13.3 g

26. Mushroom-Egg Casserole

Preparation Time: 10 minutes

Cooking Time: 30 minutes

Servings: 3

Ingredients:

- ½ cup mushrooms, chopped
- ½ yellow onion, diced
- 4 eggs, beaten
- 1 tbsp coconut flakes
- ½ tsp chili pepper
- 1 oz Cheddar cheese, shredded
- 1 tsp canola oil

Directions

Put canola oil into a skillet and preheat well.

Add mushrooms and onion and roast for 5-8 minutes or until the vegetables are light brown.

Place cooked vegetables into the casserole mold.

Add coconut flakes, chili pepper, Cheddar cheese, and eggs and stir well.

Cook the casserole in the oven for 15 minutes at 360ºF.

Nutrition

Nutrition: Calories: 411 Fat: 17 g Fiber: 13 g Carbs: 51 g Protein: 14 g

27. Brown Rice Salad

Preparation Time: 10 minutes

Cooking Time: 0 minutes

Servings: 4

Ingredients:

- 9 oz brown rice, cooked
- 7 cups baby arugula
- 15 oz canned garbanzo beans, drained and rinsed
- 4 oz feta cheese, crumbled
- ¾ cup basil, chopped
- A pinch salt and black pepper
- 2 tbsp lemon juice
- ¼ tsp lemon zest, grated
- ¼ cup olive oil

Directions

Using a salad bowl, mix the brown rice with the arugula, the beans, and all the other ingredients. Then, toss and serve cold for breakfast.

Nutrition

Nutrition: Calories: 473 g Fat: 22 g Fiber: 7 g Carbs: 53 g Protein: 13 g

28. Olive and Milk Bread

Preparation Time: 10 minutes

Cooking Time: 50 minutes

Servings: 6

Ingredients:
- 1 cup black olives, pitted, chopped
- 1 tbsp olive oil
- ½ tsp fresh yeast
- ½ cup milk, preheated
- ½ tsp salt
- 1 tsp baking powder
- 2 cups wheat flour, whole grain
- 2 eggs, beaten
- 1 tsp sugar

 **Directions**

Using a big bowl, mix fresh yeast, sugar, and milk. Stir it until the yeast is dissolved.

Add salt, baking powder, and eggs to the mixture. Stir until homogenous, and add 1 cup of wheat flour. Mix it up until smooth.

Add the olives and remaining flour. Knead the nonsticky dough.

Put the dough into a non-sticky dough mold.

Cook the bread in the oven for 50 minutes at 350°F.

Check if the bread is baked using a toothpick. If it is dry, the bread is ready.

Take the bread away from the oven and let it chill for 10 to 15 minutes.

Remove bread from the loaf mold and slice.

 **Nutrition**

Nutrition: Calories: 238 Fat: 7.7 g Fiber: 1.9 g Carbs: 35.5 g Protein: 7.2 g

Chapter 5. Grains

29. Sesame Seed Flatbread

Preparation Time: 15 minutes

Cooking Time: 2 minutes

Servings: 2

Ingredients:
- ⅓ cup spelt flour
- ¼ tsp sea salt
- 2 tbsp lukewarm spring water
- ½ tsp sesame seeds

 **Directions**

In a bowl, add spelt flour and sea salt and mix well.

Gradually, add the water and mix until a smooth dough forms.

With a clean kitchen towel, cover the bowl and set it aside for about 30 minutes.

Divide the dough into 2 portions.

Place 1 dough portion onto a floured surface and roll into a 4-inch circle.

Sprinkle the top of the bread with a pinch of salt.

Place a non-stick crepe pan over medium-high heat until heated through.

Place 1 flatbread and cook for about ½ minutes per side.

Repeat with the remaining dough portion.

Serve immediately.

Nutrition

Nutrition: Calories: 72 Fat: 0.1 g Cholesterol: 0 mg Carbs: 14.7 g Fiber: 2.5 g Protein: 2.9 g

30. Tofu Frittata with Corn and Vegan Cheese Recipe

Preparation Time: 15 minutes

Cooking Time: 10 minutes

Servings: 4

Ingredients:

- 2 tbsp extra-virgin olive oil
- 3 links tofu, cut into quarters
- 1 small onion, diced
- Kosher salt and freshly ground black pepper
- ½ cup crumbled feta, preferably Bulgarian
- 1 jalapeño, diced
- 1 yellow bell pepper, diced
- 1 orange bell pepper, diced
- 1 ripe avocado, diced
- ½ cup cilantro leaves
- 1 ear corn then kernels cut off the cob

Directions

Adjust the broiler rack from the heat source to 10 inches, and preheat the broiler to high.

Heat oil over medium-high heat in a 12-inch skillet, until shimmering. Attach the onion and cook, stirring for about 2 minutes, until softened. Top with pepper and salt. Stir in jalapeño, bell peppers, corn, and tofu and cook for about 6 minutes until browned.

Switch to broiler and cook for around 3 minutes, until the top is set. Allow the frittata to cool a bit, then use a spatula to loosen the bottom and sides. Flip out the frittata carefully using a plate larger than the saucepan. Cut into wedges and serve with sliced cilantro and avocado.

Nutrition

Nutrition: Calories: 240 Carbs: 4 g Fat: 18 g Protein: 17 g

31. Quinoa and Wild Rice

Preparation Time: 10 minutes

Cooking Time: 18 minutes

Servings: 2

Ingredients:

- ½ cup wild rice, boiled
- 2 tbsp dried cherries
- ½ cup tricolor quinoa, uncooked
- ½ key lime, zested
- ¼ cup cherry tomato dressing, homemade

- Extra:
- ½ tsp salt, divided
- ⅛ tsp cayenne pepper
- ⅛ tsp ground cardamom
- ½ tbsp olive oil
- ½ cup spring water

Directions

Cook the quinoa, and take a medium saucepan, place it over medium heat, add oil and when hot, add quinoa and cook for 3 minutes until softened.

Pour in the water, add lime zest and all the seasonings and spices, stir until mixed, and then bring the mixture to a boil.

Then switch heat to medium-low level and simmer quinoa for 10 to 12 minutes until tender.

When done, let the quinoa cool for 10 minutes, fluff it with a fork and transfer it into a medium bowl.

Add rice and tomato dressing, stir until well mixed, add cherries and then toss until mixed.

Nutrition

Nutrition: Calories: 132, Fat: 3.5 g Protein: 4.5 g Carbs: 22 g Fiber: 2 g

32. Spelt Biscuits

Preparation Time: 10 minutes

Cooking Time: 15 minutes

Servings: 2

Ingredients:

- 1 cup spelt flour
- ½ tsp salt
- ½ tbsp baking powder
- 3 tbsp walnut butter, homemade
- 6 tbsp walnut milk, homemade

Directions

Switch on the oven, then set it to 450°F and let it preheat.

Meanwhile, place flour in a food processor, add salt, baking powder, and butter, and then pulse until the mixture resembles crumbs.

Tip the mixture into a bowl, stir in milk until the dough comes together, and then roll it into a 1-inch-thick dough.

Use a cutter to cut out biscuits, arrange them on a baking sheet, and then bake for 12 to 15 minutes until golden brown.

Nutrition

Nutrition: Calories: 240, Fat: 4 g Protein: 10 g Carbs: 56 g Fiber: 16 g

33. Herbed Wild Rice

Preparation Time: 5 minutes

Cooking Time: 45 minutes

Servings: 2

Ingredients:

- 1 cup wild rice
- ½ tsp dried basil
- ½ tsp dried thyme
- ½ tsp dried oregano
- 3 cups vegetable broth, homemade
-
- Extra:
- ½ tsp salt

Directions

Take a medium saucepan, place it over medium-high heat, add rice, pour in water, and bring it to a boil covering the pan with a lid.

Then turn the heat to a low level and simmer the rice for 40 minutes until tender.

Drain excess liquid from rice, add herbs, stir until mixed, and then serve.

Nutrition

Nutrition: Calories: 165, Fat: 0.6 g Protein: 6.5 g Carbs: 35 g Fiber: 3 g

34. Amaranth Polenta

Preparation Time: 5 minutes

Cooking Time: 15 minutes

Servings: 2

Ingredients:

- ¾ cup amaranth
- ¼ tsp onion powder
- ¼ tsp salt
- 6 tbsp walnut milk, homemade
- 1 ½ cup vegetable broth, homemade
-
- Extra:
- ⅛ tsp cayenne pepper

Directions

Take a medium pot, place it over medium heat, pour in the broth, stir in salt and then bring it to a boil.

Then switch heat to medium-low level, whisk in amaranth and then cook for 10 to 20 minutes until a slightly thick mixture comes together.

Add remaining ingredients stir until mixed and continue cooking for 5 minutes.

Serve polenta with chickpeas.

Nutrition

Nutrition: Calories: 172, Fat: 4.5 g Protein: 18.5 g

35. Banana & Walnut Bread

Preparation Time: 15 minutes

Cooking Time: 50 minutes

Servings: 10

Ingredients:

- 1 cup rye flour
- 1 cup spelt flour
- 1 tsp ground ginger
- 1 tsp ground cloves
- 10 burro bananas, peeled and mashed
- ½ cup agave nectar
- ½ cup unsweetened hemp milk
- ½ cup grapeseed oil
- ½ cup walnuts, chopped

Directions

Preheat your oven to 350ºF.

Lightly grease and flour a loaf pan.

In a bowl, add the flour, ginger, and cloves and mix well.

Add the bananas, agave nectar, hemp milk, and oil and beat until well combined.

Gently fold in the walnuts.

Place the dough into the prepared loaf pan.

Bake for approximately 50 minutes or until a wooden skewer inserted in the center of the loaf comes out clean.

Remove from the oven and place the baking sheet onto a wire rack to cool for at least 10 minutes.

Carefully invert the bread onto the rack to cool completely before serving.

With a knife, cut the bread loaf into desired-sized slices and serve.

Nutrition

Nutrition: Calories: 387 Fat: 1.5 g Cholesterol: 0 mg Carbs: 59.5 g Fiber: 8.5 g Protein: 6.3 g

36. Sesame Seed Bread

Preparation Time: 15 minutes

Cooking Time: 1 hour

Servings: 10

Ingredients:

- 4 ½ cups spelt flour
- 2 tsp sea salt
- ¼ cup agave nectar
- 2 cups spring water
- 1 tbsp sesame seeds

Directions

In the bowl of a stand mixer, place 4 cups of spelt flour and salt and mix for 10 seconds.

Add the agave nectar and mix until well combined.

Lightly coat the dough hook with a little grapeseed oil.

Add the spring water, 1 cup at a time, and mix until well combined.

Now, mix on medium speed for about 5 minutes.

Add the remaining ½ cup of flour and mix until a non-sticky dough forms.

Add the sesame seeds and stir to combine.

Place dough into a lightly greased and floured loaf pan.

Cover the loaf pan and set aside for about 1 hour.

Preheat your oven to 350ºF.

Bake for approximately 52–60 minutes or until a wooden skewer inserted in the center of the loaf comes out clean.

Remove from the oven and place the baking sheet onto a wire rack to cool for at least 10 minutes.

Carefully invert the bread onto the rack to cool completely before serving.

With a knife, cut the bread loaf into desired-sized slices and serve.

Nutrition

Nutrition: Calories: 245, Fat: 0.1 g Cholesterol: 0 mg Carbs: 46.2 g Fiber: 7.7 g Protein: 7.3 g

37. Quinoa Bread

Preparation Time: 10 minutes

Cooking Time: 25 minutes

Servings: 6

Ingredients:

- 1 cup uncooked quinoa
- ¼ tsp sea salt
- 1 cup spring water

Directions

Preheat your oven to 425ºF.

Line a round baking pan with parchment paper.

In a food processor, add all the ingredients and pulse until a pancake batter consistency is achieved.

Place the mixture into the prepared pan and with a spatula, spread in an even layer.

Bake for approximately 15 minutes.

Remove from the oven and carefully flip the bread.

Bake for approximately 6–10 minutes further or until golden brown.

Remove from the oven and place the pan onto a wire rack to cool for at least 10 minutes.

Carefully invert the bread onto the rack to cool completely before serving.

With a knife, cut the bread loaf into desired-sized slices and serve.

Nutrition

Nutrition: Calories: 104 Fat: 0.2 g Cholesterol: 0 mg Carbs: 18.2 g Fiber: 2 g Protein: 4 g

38. Quinoa & Chia Bread

Preparation Time: 10 minutes

Cooking Time: 1 ½ hour

Servings: 12

Ingredients:

- ¾ cup uncooked quinoa, soaked overnight and rinsed
- ¼ cup chia seeds, soaked in ½ cup wate overnight
- ½ tsp bicarbonate soda
- ¼ tsp sea salt
- ¼ cup grapeseed oil
- ½ cup spring water
- 1 tbsp fresh key lime juice

Directions

Preheat your oven to 320ºF.

Line a loaf of pans with parchment paper.

In a food processor, add all the ingredients: and pulse for about 3 minutes.

Place the dough into the prepared loaf pan evenly.

Bake for approximately 1½ hours or until a wooden skewer inserted in the center of the loaf comes out clean.

Remove from the oven and place the baking sheet onto a wire rack to cool for at least 10 minutes.

Carefully invert the bread onto the rack to cool completely before serving.

With a knife, cut the bread loaf into desired-sized slices and serve.

sized slices and serve.

Nutrition

Nutrition: Calories: 141 Fat: 0.7 g Cholesterol: 0 mg Carbs: 16.9 g Fiber: 2.6 g Protein: 4 g

39. Three Flours Bread

Preparation Time: 10 minutes

Cooking Time: 1 Hour

Servings: 12

Ingredients:

- 3 cups quinoa flour
- 2 cups chickpeas flour
- 1 cup spelt flour
- 3 cups Perrier water
- 3 tbsp fresh key lime juice
- 3 tbsp onion powder
- 1 tbsp sea salt

Directions

Preheat your oven to 350ºF.

Lightly grease a bread loaf pan.

In a bowl, place all ingredients and with a wooden spoon, mix until thick dough forms.

Pour the mixture into the prepared loaf pan evenly.

Bake for approximately ¾–1 hour or until a wooden skewer inserted in the center of the loaf comes out clean.

Remove from the oven and place the baking

sheet onto a wire rack to cool for at least 10 minutes.

Carefully invert the bread onto the rack to cool completely before serving.

With a knife, cut the bread loaf into desired-sized slices and serve.

Nutrition

Nutrition: Calories: 210 Fat: 0.1 g Cholesterol: 0 mg Carbs: 34.2 g Fiber: 5 g Protein: 8.8 g

40. Herb Bread

Preparation Time: 15 minutes

Cooking Time: 50 minutes

Servings: 10

Ingredients:

- 4 cups chickpea flour
- 1 tbsp sea salt
- 1 tbsp onion powder
- 1 tsp dried basil
- 1 tsp dried thyme
- 1 tsp dried oregano
- ½ cup date syrup
- 3 tbsp grapeseed oil
- 1–1 ½ cup spring water

Directions

Preheat your oven to 350ºF.

Grease a 9x5-inch loaf pan

In a bowl, add chickpea flour, sea salt, garlic powder, and herbs and mix well.

Add the date syrup, oil and 1 cup of the spring water and gently stir to combine. (If the mixture is too thick, add more water, ¼ cup at a Time).

Place the mixture into the prepared loaf pan.

Bake for approximately 50–60 minutes or until a wooden skewer inserted in the center of the loaf comes out clean.

Remove from the oven and place the baking sheet onto a wire rack to cool for at least 10 minutes.

Carefully invert the bread onto the rack to cool

Nutrition

Nutrition: Calories: 224, Fat: 0.7 g Cholesterol: 0 mg Carbs: 34.2 g Fiber: 4.1 g Protein: 9.9 g

41. Herbed Flatbread

Directions:

Preparation Time: 15 minutes

Cooking Time: 36 minutes

Servings: 6

- 2 cups spelt flour
- 2 tsp dried oregano, crushed
- 2 tsp dried basil, crushed
- 1 tbsp sea salt
- ¼ tsp cayenne powder
- 2 tbsp grapeseed oil
- ¾ cup spring water

Directions

In a bowl, add the flour, herbs, and spices and mix well.

Add the oil and ½ cup of water and mix until well combined.

Slowly, add the remaining water and mix until a ball of dough forms.

Place the dough onto a lightly floured surface and with your hands, gently knead the dough for about 5 minutes.

Divide the dough into 6 portions.

Place 1 dough portion onto a floured surface and roll into a 4-inch circle.

Sprinkle the top of the bread with a pinch of salt.

Heat a nonstick crepe pan over medium-high heat and cook the flatbread for about 5–6 minutes, flipping occasionally.

Repeat with remaining dough portions.

Serve immediately.

Nutrition

Nutrition: Calories: 215, Fat: 0.4 g Cholesterol: 0 mg Carbs: 33.7 g Fiber: 5.6 g Protein: 5.4 g

42. Mushroom Risotto

Preparation Time: 5 minutes

Cooking Time: 1 hour and 25 minutes

Servings: 4

Ingredients:
- 4 oz sliced mushrooms
- ¼ onion, chopped
- 1 cup wild rice
- 1 tbsp grapeseed oil
- 2 cups vegetable broth, homemade
-
- Extra:
- ⅓ tsp salt
- ¼ tsp cayenne pepper

Directions

Take a medium pot, place it over medium heat add oil and when hot, add onion and mushroom and then cook for 4 to 5 minutes until mushrooms have turned golden brown and the liquid in the pan has evaporated.

Add rice, stir until mixed, cook for 1 minute, and then stir in salt and cayenne pepper.

Pour in the broth, switch the heat to the low level and then cook the rice for 1 hour and 20 minutes until rice is tender.

Nutrition

Nutrition: Calories: 133, Fat: 1.3 g Protein: 4.5 g Carbs: 25.2 g Fiber: 2.4 g

43. Mushroom Wild Rice Stir-fry

Preparation Time: 5 minutes

Servings: 3

Cooking Time: 15 minutes

Ingredients:

- ½ of medium white onion, peeled, diced
- 10 button mushrooms, sliced
- 1 cup Kale leaves
- 2 cups cooked wild rice
-
- Extra:
- 1 tbsp grapeseed oil
- ⅔ tsp salt
- ¼ tsp cayenne pepper

Directions

Take a large skillet pan, place it over medium heat, add oil and when hot, add onion and then cook for 4 minutes until tender.

Add mushrooms, stir until mixed and cook for 4 minutes until mushrooms have almost tender.

Add wild rice and Kale into the pan, season with salt and cayenne pepper, stir until mixed and then cook for 5 minutes until leaves wilt.

Nutrition

Nutrition: Calories: 234, Fat: 13 g Protein: 6 g Carbs: 22 g Fiber: 6 g

44. Delicious Quinoa Bowl

Preparation Time: 5 minutes

Cooking Time: 3 minutes

Servings: 2

Ingredients:

- ⅓ cup quinoa, cooked
- ¼ cup cherry tomatoes, quartered
- ½ green bell pepper, chopped
- ⅓ cup basil leaves
- 1 tbsp grapeseed oil
-
- Extra:
- ¼ tsp salt
- ⅛ tsp cayenne pepper

Directions

Take a pan, place it over medium heat, add oil and when hot, add cherry tomatoes and bell pepper and cook for 2 to 3 minutes until tender-crisp.

Take a medium bowl, place cooked quinoa in it, add tomatoes and bell pepper mixture, and then add basil leaves.

Season with salt and cayenne pepper, stir until mixed and then serve.

Nutrition

Nutrition: Calories: 141, Fat: 6.2 g Protein: 6.5 g Carbs: 32 g Fiber: 4.1 g

45. Chickpea Loaf

Preparation Time: 10 minutes

Cooking Time: 45 minutes

Servings: 4

Ingredients:

- ¼ cup spelt flour
- 1 ½ cup chickpeas, cooked
- ¾ cup diced onions
- ¼ cup minced basil
- ½ cup sliced white mushrooms
-
- Extra:
- 1 red bell pepper, cored, diced
- 1 tbsp grapeseed oil
- 1 tbsp and ¼ tsp granulated onion, homemade
- ⅛ tsp dried thyme
- ½ tsp sea salt and more as needed
- ⅓ tsp dried sage
- ¼ tsp cayenne pepper and more as needed
- ¼ tsp dried oregano

Directions

Switch on the oven, then set it to 350°F and let it preheat.

Meanwhile, take a large skillet pan, place it over medium-high heat, add oil to it and when hot, add onion, pepper, and mushroom and then cook for 3 minutes or until it begins to tender.

Add minced basil into the pan, stir until mixed, remove the pan from heat, add all the seasonings and then stir until mixed.

Place chickpeas in a food processor, pulse until coarsely chopped, and then transfer into a medium bowl.

Add the cooked vegetable mixture along with the remaining ingredients stir until well mixed and then spoon into a greased loaf pan.

Bake the loaf for 30 to 40 minutes until firm and cooked, cool it slightly, cut it into slices and then serve.

Nutrition

Nutrition: Calories: 268.7, Fat: 6.2 g Protein: 10.3 g Carbs: 46 g Fiber: 9.4 g

46. Kamut Porridge with Dates

Preparation Time: 5 minutes

Servings: 2

Cooking Time: 15 minutes

Ingredients:

- 1 cup dates, pitted, chopped
- 1 cup rolled Kamut flakes
- ⅛ tsp salt
- 2 cups spring water

Directions

Place Kamut flakes in a small saucepan, pour in the water, and let soak overnight.

Then stir in salt, place the pan over medium-high heat and bring the mixture to a slow boil.

Switch heat to medium-low level and then

continue cooking for 10 minutes or more until all the liquid has been absorbed.

Remove pan from heat, add dates into the porridge and then stir until mixed.

Divide porridge between 2 bowls, drizzle with agave syrup if needed, and then serve.

Nutrition

Nutrition: Calories: 132, Fat: 1 g Protein: 0.3 g Carbs: 30.2 g Fiber: 2 g

47. Kamut Pasta

Preparation Time: 5 minutes

Servings: 2

Cooking Time: 0 minutes

Ingredients:

- ½ cup sliced zucchini
- 2 cups cooked spelt pasta
- ¼ cup diced onions
- ½ cup diced green bell peppers
- ¼ cup cherry tomatoes, cut in half
-
- Extra:
- 2 tbsp olives
- ½ cup alkaline sauce, homemade

Directions

Take a large bowl, place all the ingredients in it and then toss until well coated.

Nutrition

Nutrition: Calories: 143.7, Fat: 1.8 g Protein: 4.5 g Carbs: 1 g Fiber: 4.8 g

48. Walnut Milk Bread

Preparation Time: 10 minutes

Cooking Time: 45 minutes

Servings: 12

Ingredients:

- 4 cups spelt flour plus ½ cup more for dusting
- 1 tsp baking soda
- 1 ½ tsp fine sea salt
- 1 tbsp agave nectar
- ½ cup homemade walnut milk
- 3 tbsp grapeseed oil
- ¾–1 cup spring water

Directions

Preheat your oven to 375°F.

Line an 8x4x3-inch loaf pans with greased parchment paper.

In a large bowl, add the flour, baking soda, and salt and mix well.

Add the walnut milk, oil, and ¾ cup of water and mix until well combined.

Dust a smooth surface with some spelt flour.

Place the dough onto the surface and gently roll it around to coat it with the flour.

With your clean hands, knead the dough for about 2–3 minutes, adding flour in small amounts until a dough ball forms.

Place the dough into the prepared loaf pan.

Bake for approximately 45 minutes or until a wooden skewer inserted in the center of the loaf comes out clean.

Remove from the oven and place the baking sheet onto a wire rack to cool for at least 10 minutes.

Carefully invert the bread onto the rack to cool completely before serving.

With a knife, cut the bread loaf into desired-sized slices and serve.

Nutrition

Nutrition: Calories: 197 Fat: 0.3 g Cholesterol: 0 mg Carbs: 30.7 g Fiber: 5.4 g Protein: 5.4 g

Chapter 6. Lunch Recipes

49. Vegetarian Spanish Mixed Green Salad

Preparation Time: 15 minutes

Cooking Time: 25 minutes

Servings: 3

Ingredients:

- ½ Spanish onion
- 10-12 green olives
- 2 cups Boston lettuce
- 2 tomatoes
- 1 cup baby spinach
- 2 cups romaine lettuce

Directions

Dressing:

3 tbsp olive oil

Sea salt and black pepper

1 tbsp lemon juice

Combine all of the dressing components in a mixing bowl and whisk until thoroughly combined.

Toss with salad well before eating.

Nutrition

Nutrition: Calories: 240 Carbs: 16 g Protein: 25 g Total Fat: 8 g

50. Vegetarian Spanish Rice Dinner

Preparation Time: 15 minutes

Cooking Time: 25 minutes

Servings: 3

Ingredients:

- ⅛ tsp pepper
- ⅛ tsp hot pepper sauce
- ½ tsp ground mustard
- ¼ tsp garlic powder
- 1 tsp salt
- 1 tsp Worcestershire sauce
- 1 tbsp onion

- 1 can stewed tomatoes
- 1 can green beans
- 1 ½ cup cooked rice

Directions

Steam beef when no pinker in a large frying pan; clean.

Add the rest of the ingredients and stir to combine.

Raise the temperature to high and bring the mixture to a boil.

Reduce to a low-heat environment, cover, and cook for 510 minutes, or until thoroughly cooked.

Nutrition

Nutrition: Calories: 282 Carbs: 8.2 g Protein: 24.4 g Total Fat: 15.4 g

51. Spanish Garlic Mushrooms

Preparation Time: 15 minutes

Cooking Time: 25 minutes

Servings: 3

Ingredients:

- 1 tbsp lemon juice
- 2 tbsp fresh parsley
- Salt to taste
- ½ cup white wine
- 4 garlic cloves
- 2 lb mushrooms

- 2 tbsp olive oil

Directions

In a large skillet over medium heat, add the oil over moderate flame.

Cook the mushrooms for about 4 minutes, turning the pan frequently.

Heat, for about 13 more minutes until crisp, adding the garlic, cayenne pepper, salt and pepper.

Add the tarragon to mix well.

Serve the aioli and lime wedges along with the mushrooms.

Nutrition

Nutrition: Calories: 284 Carbs: 1.4 g Protein: 24.2 g Total Fat: 17 g

52. Greek Vegetarian Stuffed Zucchini

Preparation Time: 15 minutes

Cooking Time: 25 minutes

Servings: 3

Ingredients:

- 8 pitted Kalamata olives
- ½ cup crumbled feta cheese
- 1 cup cooked quinoa
- 1 cup diced plum tomatoes
- 4 medium zucchinis
- ¾ tsp smoked paprika

- 1 tbsp chopped fresh oregano
- ¾ cup chopped onion
- 1 tbsp garlic
- ¼ tsp salt
- 1 tbsp extra-virgin olive oil
- ½ tsp ground pepper

Directions

Heat the oven to 350°F.

Break each zucchini in a quarter lengthwise, use a fork, and scrape much of the skin, preserving ½-inch thick cores.

Chop a quarter of the flesh thinly sliced; waste the remainder flesh or save it for some purpose.

Cover a baking dish with the zucchini pellets; brush with salt and black pepper.

Bake for 15 to 20 minutes before the zucchini begins to soften.

In the meantime, over a moderate flame, heat the oil in a large skillet.

Add the sliced zucchini, onions, cloves, paprika, and 2 tablespoons of oregano; boil for approximately 3 minutes, stirring regularly, until the onion begins to soften.

Stir in the quinoa, olives, tomatoes, and feta, and extract from the heat. Split the zucchini cores equally.

Turn to broil the oven and put a rack 8 inches away from the heat.

Broil the cores of packed zucchini till the edges are finely browned for 4 to 6 minutes.

Stir with 1 teaspoon of the leftover oregano.

Nutrition

Nutrition: Calories: 284 Carbs: 1.4 g Protein: 24.2 g Total Fat: 17 g

53. Greek Vegetarian Soutzoukakia

Preparation Time: 15 minutes

Cooking Time: 25 minutes

Servings: 3

Ingredients:

- For the Oriental Meatballs:
- Pepper to taste
- 200 g all-purpose flour
- 1 tbsp parsley
- Salt to taste
- 500 g chickpeas
- 1 clove garlic
- 1 bunch mint
- 3 tbsp olive oil
- ½ lemon, juiced
- 3 onions, dry
- 1 tsp cumin, powder
- 1 lemon, zest
- 1 tbsp baking powder
-
- For the Sauce:
- Salt to taste
- Pepper to taste
- 1 tbsp tomato paste
- 3 tomatoes
- 1 clove garlic
- 1 tsp granulated sugar
- 2 tbsp olive oil
- 1 tsp oregano
- 1 chili pepper, dried
- 1 onion, dry

- 1 onion, dry
- 3 bay leaves
- 1 stick cinnamon

Directions

Put a reasonable quantity of water in a jar with the chickpeas and continue cooking.

Wash them before they break for twelve hours or overnight.

Dump, washed off when prepared.

Move and pulse a bit to a mixing bowl, ensuring you do not produce a paste.

Put the olive oil, baking soda, cilantro, lime zest, lime juice, diced onion, grated cloves, coarsely chopped mint, salt, and black pepper in a bowl and transfer to the mixture. Rigorously blend.

Form the combination into oval-shaped meatballs and excavate in the starch.

Over moderate to low heat, put a large pan and heat the oil, and let it get heated. Insert the meatballs cautiously in quantities and cook until they become golden.

To drain, switch to a cooking pan filled with paper towels.

Put the olive oil, the finely diced onion, the bay leaf, the spices, the dried oregano, the mustard, the hot pepper, the crushed garlic cloves, the granulated sugar, and the tomato sauce in a shallow bowl.

Garnish with the grated onion, salt, and black pepper.

Reduce the heat and add the crispy meatballs to the dish. Cover and cook with a cap for 10 minutes.

Present with boiling basmati rice, rosemary, canola oil, and clean oregano.

Nutrition

Nutrition: Calories: 371 Carbs: 1.7 g Protein: 33.7 g Total Fat: 25.1 g

54. Lean and Green "Macaroni

Preparation Time: 15 minutes

Cooking Time: 25 minutes

Servings: 3

Ingredients:

- 2 tbsp yellow onion, diced
- 5 oz 9597% lean ground beef
- 2 tbsp light thousand island dressing
- ⅛ tsp apple cider vinegar
- ⅛ tsp onion powder
- 3 cups Romaine lettuce, shredded
- 2 tbsp low-fat cheddar cheese, shredded
- 1 oz dill pickle slices
- 1 tsp sesame seeds

Directions

Sauté the onions for less than a minute before adding the beef. Sauté the beef for 5 minutes, stirring continuously.

Add in the Thousand Island dressing, apple cider vinegar, and onion powder.

Close the lid and continue cooking for 6 minutes. Then let simmer by removing the lid until the sauce thickens.

In a bowl, place the lettuce at the bottom and

pour in the beef. Layer with cheddar cheese, and pickles. Sprinkle with sesame on top.

Nutrition

Nutrition: Calories: 119, Protein: 10.8 g Carbs: 4.4 g Fat: 2.1 g Sugar: 2.5 g

55. Lean and Green Broccoli Taco

Preparation Time: 15 minutes

Cooking Time: 25 minutes

Servings: 3

Ingredients:

- 4 oz 9597% lean ground beef
- ¼ cup Roma tomatoes, chopped
- ¼ tsp garlic powder
- ¼ tsp onion powder
- 1 ¼ cup broccoli, cut into bite-sized pieces
- A pinch of red pepper flakes
- 1 oz low-sodium cheddar cheese, shredded

Directions

Place 3 tablespoons of water in a pan and heat over medium flame. Water sautés the beef and tomatoes for 5 minutes until the tomatoes are wilted. Add in the garlic and onion powder and stir for another 3 minutes.

Add the broccoli and close the lid. Cook for another 5 minutes.

Garnish with red pepper flakes and cheddar cheese on top.

Nutrition

Nutrition: Calories: 97, Protein: 9.9 g Carbs: 2.6 g Fat: 1.7 g Sugar: 0.9 g

56. Lean and Green Crunchy Chicken Tacos

Preparation Time: 15 minutes

Cooking Time: 25 minutes

Servings: 3

Ingredients:

- ½ cup low-sodium chicken stock
- 2 chicken breasts, minced
- 1 red onion, chopped
- 1 clove garlic, minced
- 3 plum tomatoes, chopped
- 1 tsp cumin powder
- 1 tsp cinnamon powder
- 1 tsp ground coriander
- 1 red onion, chopped
- ½ red chili, chopped
- 1 tbsp lime juice
- Meat from 1 ripe avocado
- 1 cucumber, sliced into thick rounds

Directions

Place a tablespoon of chicken stock in a pan and heat over medium flame. Water sautés the chicken, onion, garlic, and tomatoes for 4 minutes or until the tomatoes have wilted.

Season with cumin, cinnamon, and coriander. Reduce the heat to low and cook for another 5 minutes. Set aside and allow cooling.

In a bowl, mix the onion, chili, lime juice, and mashed avocado. This is the salsa.

Scoop the salsa and top it on sliced cucumber. Top with cooked chicken.

Nutrition

Nutrition: Calories: 313, Protein: 31.8 g Carbs: 14.9 g Fat: 3.8 g Sugar: 5 g

57. Cauliflower with Kale Pesto

Preparation Time: 15 minutes

Cooking Time: 25 minutes

Servings: 3

Ingredients:

- 3 cups cauliflower, cut into florets
- 3 cups raw kale, stems removed
- 2 cups fresh basil
- 2 tbsp extra virgin olive oil
- 3 tbsp lemon juice
- 3 cloves garlic
- ¼ tsp salt

Directions

Put enough water in a pot and bring to a boil over medium flame. Blanch the cauliflower for 2 minutes. Drain then place in a bowl of ice-cold water for 5 minutes. Drain again.

In a blender, add the rest of the ingredients. Pulse until smooth.

Pour the pesto over the cooked cauliflower.

Nutrition

Nutrition: Calories: 41, Protein: 1.8 g Carbs: 5 g Fat: 5.3 g Sugar: 1.4 g

58. Lean and Green Chicken Chili

Preparation Time: 15 minutes

Cooking Time: 25 minutes

Servings: 3

Ingredients:

- 1 lb boneless skinless chicken breast, chopped
- 1 tsp ground cumin
- 1 cup chopped poblano pepper
- ½ cup chopped onion
- 1 clove garlic, minced
- 2 cups low-sodium chicken broth
- 1 cup rehydrated pinto beans
- 1 cup chopped tomatoes
- 2 tbsp minced cilantro

Directions

Place all ingredients except the cilantro in a pressure cooker.

Close the lid and set the vent to the sealing position.

Cook on high for 45 minutes until the beans are soft.

Garnish with cilantro before serving

Nutrition

Nutrition: Calories: 229, Protein: 26.1 g Carbs: 23.9 g Fat: 2 g Sugar: 2.2 g

59. Lean and Green Broccoli Alfredo

Preparation Time: 15 minutes

Cooking Time: 25 minutes

Servings: 3

Ingredients:

- 2 heads broccoli, cut into florets
- 2 tbsp lemon juice, freshly squeezed
- ½ cup cashew, soaked for 2 hours in water then drained
- 2 tbsp white miso, low sodium
- 2 tsp Dijon mustard
- Freshly cracked black pepper

Directions

Boil water in a pot over medium flame. Blanch the broccoli for 2 minutes then places it in a bowl of iced water. Drain.

In a food processor, place the remaining ingredients and pulse until smooth.

Pour the Alfredo sauce over the broccoli. Toss to coat with the sauce.

Nutrition

Nutrition: Calories: 359, Protein: 10.6 g Carbs: 50.2 g Fat: 8.4 g Sugar: 2.4 g

60. Lean and Green Steak Machine

Preparation Time: 15 minutes

Cooking Time: 25 minutes

Servings: 3

Ingredients:

- 1 lb boneless skinless chicken breast, chopped
- 1 tsp ground cumin
- 1 cup chopped poblano pepper
- ½ cup chopped onion
- 1 clove garlic, minced
- 2 cups low-sodium chicken broth
- 1 cup rehydrated pinto beans
- 1 cup chopped tomatoes
- 2 tbsp minced cilantro

Directions

Place a tablespoon of chicken stock in a pan and heat over medium flame. Water sautés the chicken, onion, garlic, and tomatoes for 4 minutes or until the tomatoes have wilted.

Season with cumin, cinnamon, and coriander. Reduce the heat to low and cook for another 5 minutes. Set aside and allow cooling.

In a bowl, mix the onion, chili, lime juice, and mashed avocado. This is the salsa.

Scoop the salsa and top it on sliced cucumber. Top with cooked chicken.

Nutrition

Nutrition: Calories: 313, Protein: 31.8 g Carbs: 14.9 g Fat: 3.8 g Sugar: 5 g

61. Lean and Green Crockpot Chili

Preparation Time: 15 minutes

Cooking Time: 25 minutes

Servings: 3

Ingredients:

- 1 lb boneless skinless chicken breasts, cut into strips
- ½ cup chopped onion
- 2 tsp ground cumin
- 1 tsp minced garlic
- ½ tsp chili powder
- Salt and pepper to taste
- 1 ½ cup water

Directions

Place all ingredients in a pot.

Mix all ingredients until combined.

Close the lid and turn on the heat to medium.

Bring to a boil and allow to simmer for 45 minutes or until the beans are cooked.

Serve with chopped cilantro on top.

Nutrition

Nutrition: Calories: 84, Protein: 13.4 g Carbs: 3.6 g Fat: 1.7 g Sugar: 0.8 g

62. Buffalo Cauliflower Bites

Preparation Time: 15 minutes

Cooking Time: 25 minutes

Servings: 3

Ingredients:

- Cauliflower florets, 5 ½ cups or cooked, 4 ½ cups (9 Greens)
- Buffalo hot sauce, divided, ½ cup, (4 Condiments)
- Garlic powder, ¼ tsp, (½ Condiment)
- Blue cheese or light ranch dressing, divided, 6 tbsp, (3 Healthy Fat)

Directions

Put ¼ cup of garlic powder and hot buffalo sauce in the cauliflower florets. Toss to coat it with the dressing.

For easy cleanup, use cooking spray or put parchment paper (do not use wax paper) on the base of the air fryer. After setting the air fryer to 360, cook for 13 to 15 minutes, stirring every 5 minutes.

In a medium size bowl, put the cooked cauliflower and add the excess ¼ cup of Buffalo Hot Sauce. Coat by tossing. Relish with 2 tablespoons of blue cheese or light ranch dressing!

If using the oven, at 450°F, cook for 20 min, mixing when half done.

Nutrition

Nutrition: Calories: 14, Protein: 1.03 g Fat: 0.22 g Carbs: 2.67 g

63. Lovely Faux Mac and Cheese

Preparation Time: 15 minutes

Cooking Time: 25 minutes

Servings: 3

Ingredients:

- 5 cups cauliflower florets
- Sunflower seeds and pepper to taste
- 1 cup coconut almond milk
- ½ cup vegetable broth
- 2 tbsp coconut flour, sifted
- 1 organic egg, beaten
- 1 cup cashew cheese

Directions

Preheat your oven to 350°F.

Season florets with sunflower seeds and steam until firm.

Place florets in a greased ovenproof dish.

Heat coconut almond milk over medium heat in a skillet, make sure to season the oil with sunflower seeds and pepper.

Stir in broth and add coconut flour to the mix, stir.

Cook until the sauce begins to bubble.

Remove heat and add beaten egg.

Pour the thick sauce over the cauliflower and mix in the cheese.

Bake for 3045 minutes.

Serve and enjoy!

Nutrition

Nutrition: Calories: 229, Fat: 14 g Carbs: 9 g Protein: 15 g

64. Greek Steamed Vegetable Bowls

Preparation Time: 15 minutes

Cooking Time: 25 minutes

Servings: 3

Ingredients:

For the Steamed Vegetables:
- Olive oil
- Salt and black pepper
- 2 medium bell peppers
- 8 oz mushrooms
- 2 medium zucchinis
- 1 red onion

For the Bowls:
- Salt and black pepper to taste
- Pita chips
- Fresh dill and basil
- Avocado Tzatziki
- 2 cups cooked farro
- ½ cup Kalamata olives
- ½ cup crumbled feta cheese
- 15 oz chickpeas
- 1 cup halved grape tomatoes
- 1 cucumber

For the Lemon Dressing:
- 1 tsp dried oregano
- Kosher salt and black pepper to taste
- ½ tsp Dijon mustard
- 2 cloves garlic
- ½ cup olive oil
- 2 tbsp lemon juice
- ½ cup red wine vinegar

- 5 cups cauliflower florets
- Sunflower seeds and pepper to taste
- 1 cup coconut almond milk
- ½ cup vegetable broth

Directions

Heat the Steam to high.

Sprinkle olive oil over the veggies and add salt and pepper.

Roast the veggies until crispy and Steam marks emerge, flipping once.

Take it from the fire.

Mix the olive oil, Dijon mustard, white wine vinegar, lime juice, cloves, oregano, pepper, and salt in a shallow saucepan or container to make the coating.

Thinly slice the roasted veggies to fill the bowls.

Cover each dish with the Steamed peppers, cucumber, chickpeas, Kalamata olives, tomatoes, and feta cheese, and split the farro into 4 cups.

Garnish with spices and, to taste, sprinkle with salt. Sprinkle and eat with tzatziki and pita chips with seasoning.

Nutrition

Nutrition: Calories: 385, Carbs: 48.5 g Protein: 24.5 g Total Fat: 8.5 g

65. Greek Veggie Balls with Tahini Lemon Sauce

Preparation Time: 15 minutes

Cooking Time: 25 minutes

Servings: 3

Ingredients:

- 1 large lemon
- 2 (15-oz) cans dry peas
- ½ cup whole wheat breadcrumbs
- ½ cup nut meal
- 1 medium red onion
- Pinch sea salt
- ¼ cup ground flax seeds
- 3 cloves garlic
- 1 tbsp oregano
- ½ tsp black pepper
- 5 soft dates
- ½ cup fresh parsley
- 1 tsp fennel seeds
- ¼ cup sliced sundried tomatoes

Tahini Lemon Sauce:
- Water
- Smoked paprika
- 2 cloves garlic
- ¼ tsp black pepper
- 1 large lemon
- ½ cup tahini

Directions

Position the spring onions, parsley, cloves, oregano, sundried tomatoes, dates, fennel seeds, salt, and black pepper in the spice grinder bag. Work until finely chopped.

In the food processor, add the flax seeds, corn flour, almond flour, and lime juice and pulse until mixed.

Insert the black-eyed pods into the food processor till the beans are crushed, though not purified, for a few seconds.

Take the mixture out of the food processor and cool it for thirty minutes.

In the meantime, mix all the tahini with lime juice, cloves, and black pepper to create Tahini Citrus Sauce.

Add more water, according to the ideal consistency, to form a delicious sauce.

Spray with paprika, which has been smoked.

Preheat the furnace to 375 F.

Use your palms to roll vegetarian balls into 24 golf-sized balls, and put them on a cookie dish coated with cooking spray. Position it on the oven's top shelf.

Cook for 60 minutes, until the vegetarian balls, are baked, and the surface is lightly browned.

Use Tahini Citrus Sauce to serve.

Nutrition

Nutrition: Calories: 433, Carbs: 10 g Protein: 38 g Total Fat: 26 g

66. Briam Greek Roasted Vegetables

Preparation Time: 15 minutes

Cooking Time: 25 minutes

Servings: 3

Ingredients:

- 1 can diced tomatoes
- 3 sprigs thyme
- ½ tsp salt
- ¼ tsp ground black pepper
- 1 large potato
- 1 cloves garlic minced
- 1 large tomato
- ½ cup extra virgin olive oil
- 1 tsp oregano
- 1 zucchini
- 1 red onion
- 1 eggplant

Directions

Begin with the veggies getting cut.

For slicing through circular forms, you can either choose a mandolin cutter or a razor blade.

To make a lovely Briam and vegetables to bake uniformly, try to choose veggies identical in volume.

Add the cut vegetables to a big bowl and stir and rain with the vegetable oil.

Add the oregano, garlic, pepper, and salt.

Give a decent mix to all so that the vegetables are prepared well.

Add the tomato sauce and ½ cup of water to an ovenproof pan. Then organize, in lines, the seasoned veggies.

In the blending cup, if there is any coconut oil remaining, pour it over the veggies.

Mold the baking sheet with foil and put it in an oven, and bake.

Cook for thirty minutes at 390°F (200°C), test if the vegetables are tender, and cover the foil.

Roast for another 1020 minutes to minimize the fluid and the veggies get their golden-brown hue.

To get the vegetables to caramelize a little, you might want to put the dish underneath the Steam for 5 minutes.

Serve with olives, feta cheese, and moldy rolls.

Nutrition

Nutrition: Calories: 117, Carbs: 5.8 g Protein: 13.9 g Total Fat: 3.7 g

67. Yemista
(Stuffed Peppers and Tomatoes)

Preparation Time: 15 minutes

Cooking Time: 25 minutes

Servings: 3

Ingredients:

- 4 potatoes
- ½ cup toasted breadcrumbs
- ½ cup olive oil
- Salt and pepper
- 2 tbsp tomato paste
- 1 tsp cinnamon
- ½ cup parsley
- 1 tbsp dried oregano
- 4 large tomatoes
- ¼ cup fresh mint

- 3 cloves garlic
- ½ cup lean mince
- 1 medium onion
- 4 large red peppers

Directions

Heat the oven to 180°C.

Trim the ends off between 12 cm from the edge of the tomatoes and peppers.

Strip the juice from the tomatoes and peppers.

Slice the onions.

Finely cut the cloves and sauté this in a bowl with onions.

Transfer the pulp as well as the other spices and herbs from the tomato.

Add the paste of tomatoes.

Cover the solution with the veggies and swap the tops.

With the roasted potatoes, cover the veggies.

Sprinkle with oil appropriately.

Spray with breadcrumbs and end with salt and black pepper.

Nutrition

Nutrition: Calories: 268, Carbs: 12.6 g Protein: 41.7 g

68. Greek Vegetarian Meatballs

Preparation Time: 15 minutes

Cooking Time: 25 minutes

Servings: 3

Ingredients:

- 2 tbsp tahini
- 3 tbsp mixture of parsley, mint, and dill
- 2 ½ tsp fresh oregano
- ½ tsp red pepper flake
- 1 cup Quinoa
- ½ cup diced shallot
- Salt and pepper to taste
- 4 tbsp olive oil
- 3 cloves garlic
- 1 (15 oz) can black beans

Directions

Heat the oven to 350°F.

On a parchment-lined baking tray, position the dry kidney beans and cook for 1015 minutes till the beans look broken and sound dry to the touch.

Take them from the furnace and raise the heat of the oven to 370°F.

Over medium-high heat, heat a large pan.

Add 2 tablespoons of olive oil, cloves, and parsley once it is warmed.

Sauté for 3 minutes, or until transparent and moderately soft, stirring regularly.

For later usage, remove from the heat and reserve the bowl.

In a mixing bowl, add kidney beans alongside cloves, parsley, salt, black pepper, pepper flake, ore-gano, and process a few times into a slim meal, becoming cautious not to mix thoroughly.

When squeezed between your fingertips, insert the quinoa, rice, tahini, chopped parsley, basil, and dill, and rotate to mix until a contoured dough shape.

Add a little more starch and shake to mix, whether it is too tacky or muddy.

Squeeze out heaping volumes of 11 ½ tablespoons and shape carefully using your palms into tiny pieces.

Patting these first and tossing them afterward. Place in a dish and chill in the fridge for fifteen mi-nutes.

Chilling is acceptable, but during skillet frying, it means the meatball holds together longer.

In a small container, put the remaining ¼ of a cup of starch.

Reheat the pan and transfer the remaining olive oil to the pan.

Brush the meatballs with powder and return them to the skillet and sauté for a few minutes, rota-ting the meatballs slightly to either surface to get a soft crust.

Then move to the oven and cook for 20 minutes or until the sides are nicely browned and gently dry to the fingertips.

Nutrition

Nutrition: Calories: 258, Carbs: 7.3 g Protein: 28 g Total Fat: 13.4 g

69. Greek Lasagna Vegetarian

Directions:

Preparation Time: 15 minutes

Cooking Time: 25 minutes

Servings: 3

Ingredients:

- Tomato Sauce
- ½ tsp black pepper
- 3 tbsp dill
- ½ cup chopped Kalamata olive
- 2 tsp salt
- 3 tbsp olive oil
- 2 tsp marjoram, dried
- 5 cups tomatoes
- 5 garlic cloves, minced
- 2 cups chopped onions
-
- Filling:
- 3 cups grated feta cheese
- ½ lb uncooked lasagna noodles
- 2 cups cottage cheese
- 1 tsp ground fennel
- Olive oil, for brushing
- 3 eggs, beaten
- 1 large eggplant

Directions

Heat the oil slightly over medium-high heat in a frying pan.

Insert the onions and sauté for about 5 minutes, stirring regularly before the liquids have started to come out of the onions.

Mix in the cloves and marjoram till the onions are transparent, and sauté.

Insert the tomatoes, cover them, and get them to a boil. Then reduce the flame, only enough to hold a spot, to moderate low.

Olives, pepper, and salt are added. Before preparing the lasagna for the perfect taste, insert the dill.

Preheat a 400°F furnace. Oil the broad baking sheet gently.

Place the eggplant circles on a baking tray as the sauce softly simmers—brush olive oil on them.

Cook for about fifteen minutes, exposed.

Replace the oven's eggplant and turn the heat down to 350F.

In the meantime, blend all the eggs, fennel, cottage cheese, and 1 cup of feta cheese in a bowl and whisk.

Nutrition

Nutrition: Calories: 257, Carbs: 10 g Protein: 29 g Total Fat: 10 g

70. Greek Style Baked Feta

Preparation Time: 15 minutes

Cooking Time: 25 minutes

Servings: 3

Ingredients:

- Fresh mint leaves
- Crusty bread
- Extra virgin olive oil
- 8 oz feta cheese
- ½ tsp red pepper flakes
- 4 fresh thyme sprigs
- ½ cup cherry tomatoes
- 2 tsp oregano
- 2 tsp butter & ½ red onion
- ½ green bell pepper

Directions

Preheat oven to 400°F and modify a tray in the center.

Organize the onions, green peppers, and grape tomatoes in the lower part of a ramekin or stove dish.

Spray some of the new thyme with 1 teaspoon of oregano, and chili flakes, and apply most of it. Drizzle some extra virgin olive oil with it.

On top of the prepared vegetables, add the feta.

Prepare the leftover dried oregano with both the feta cube, a touch of chili flakes, and whatever is left of the fresh thyme.

Sprinkle the feta with a thick layer of olive oil and ensure to rub some of the butter on the edges. Position the baking sheet on the oven's center rack and bake for 20 minutes.

Serve it with tortilla chips or Spanish toasted bread.

Nutrition

Nutrition: Calories: 152, Carbs: 2 g Protein: 6 g Total Fat: 14 g

71. Chicken Stir Fry

Preparation Time: 15 minutes

Cooking Time: 25 minutes

Servings: 3

Ingredients:

- ½ cup chicken broth, low sodium
- 12 oz skinless chicken breasts, cut into strips
- 1 cup red bell pepper, seeded and chopped
- 8 oz (1 cup) broccoli, cut into florets
- 1 tsp crushed red pepper

 **Directions**

Place a small amount of chicken broth in a saucepan. Heat over medium flame and stir in the chi-cken. Water sautés the chicken for at least 5 minutes while stirring constantly.

Place the rest of the ingredients and stir.

Cover the pan with a lid and cook for another 5 minutes.

 **Nutrition**

Nutrition: Calories: 137, Protein: 15 g Carbs: 15.4 g Fat: 1.2 g Sugar: 0.6 g

72. Lean and Green Garlic Chicken with Zoodles

Preparation Time: 15 minutes

Cooking Time: 25 minutes

Servings: 3

Ingredients:

- 1 ½ lb boneless and skinless chicken breasts, cut into bite-sized pieces
- 6 slices sundried tomatoes
- 1 tsp chopped garlic
- 1 cup low-fat plain Greek yogurt
- ½ cup chicken broth, low sodium
- ½ tsp garlic powder
- ½ tsp Italian seasoning
- 1 cup spinach, chopped
- 1 ½ cup zucchini, cut into thin noodles

 **Directions**

Place 2 tablespoons of water in a pan and heat over low medium flame.

Water sautés the chicken for 3 minutes while stirring constantly until the sides are slightly golden.

Stir in the tomatoes and garlic and stir for another 3 minutes. Add in the yogurt, chicken broth, gar-lic powder, and Italian seasoning.

Cover with a lid and allow to simmer for at least 7 minutes.

Stir in the spinach last. Cook for another 2 minutes.

Place the zucchini noodles in a deep dish and pour over the chicken. Toss the noodles to coat with the sauce.

Serve immediately.

Nutrition

Nutrition: Calories: 205, Protein: 33.3 g Carbs: 6 g Fat: 2 g Sugar: 1.2 g

73. Vegetarian Cooked Chorizo with Chick Peas and Tomatoes

Preparation Time: 15 minutes

Cooking Time: 25 minutes

Servings: 3

Ingredients:

- Salt and pepper to taste
- 3 tbsp parsley
- 2 pints cherry tomatoes
- 1 tsp smoked paprika
- 9 oz chorizo
- 2 (15 oz) cans chickpeas
- 1 onion
- 1 tbsp olive oil

Directions

In a saucepan over medium heat, steam the oil.

Sauté onion for 3 minutes, or until soft.

Toss in the chorizo.

Sauté for 30 seconds to 1 minute, or until thoroughly hot.

Combine chickpeas, grape tomatoes, and paprika in a mixing bowl.

Cook for 8 minutes, or until tomatoes are softened and liquids are boiling.

Salt and pepper to taste. Serve with a tarragon garnish.

Nutrition

Nutrition: Calories: 344, Carbs: 9 g Protein: 28 g Total Fat: 17 g

74. Mediterranean Spanish Roasted Vegetables

Preparation Time: 15 minutes

Cooking Time: 25 minutes

Servings: 3

Ingredients:

- Parmesan cheese
- Crushed red pepper
- 1 tsp dried thyme
- Salt and pepper to taste
- 8 oz baby Bella mushrooms
- Extra virgin olive oil
- ½ tbsp dried oregano
- 12 oz baby potatoes
- 2 zucchini or summer squash
- 12 large garlic cloves
- 12 oz Campari tomatoes

Directions

Preheat the oven to 375°F.

In a big mixing bowl, combine the mushrooms, vegetables, and garlic.

Drizzle a generous amount of olive oil on top.

Insert the sesame oil, tarragon, salt, and pepper to taste. Toss all together.

Take just the potatoes and lay them out on a baking pan that has been lightly greased.

Roast for 10 minutes in a preheated oven.

Remove the pan from the heat and add half the veggies and mushrooms.

Return to the oven for a final 20 minutes of roasting or until the vegetables are fork-tender.

Mix thoroughly with smashed cayenne pepper and chopped fresh Parmesan cheese.

Nutrition

Nutrition: Calories: 207, Carbs: 7.8 g Protein: 29.5 g Total Fat: 6.8 g

75. Tapas & Pinchos Vegetarian

Preparation Time: 15 minutes

Cooking Time: 25 minutes

Servings: 3

Ingredients:

Garlic Aioli Ingredients:

- ½ cup extra-virgin olive oil
- Salt to taste
- 1 tsp lemon juice
- 1 egg yolk
- 1 garlic clove
-
- Tomato Sauce Ingredients:
- 2 tsp smoked paprika
- Salt and pepper to taste
- 1 garlic clove
- 1 red jalapeno
- 1 tbsp extra-virgin olive oil
- 3 large plum tomatoes
-
- Potato Ingredients:
- 2 tbsp extra-virgin olive oil
- Salt and pepper to taste
- 1 lb potatoes
- Garnish Ingredients:
- Fresh lemon juice
- 1 tbsp parsley

Directions

Preheat the oven to 400°F.

Toss potato in canola oil and season with salt and pepper.

Position on a cookie sheet in a single sheet.

Cook for 25 to 30 minutes until its fork is ready.

In a spice grinder, puree the vegetables to make the sauce.

Add the oil to a pan.

Garlic and jalapeno peppers should be added at this stage.

Insert pureed onions, cayenne pepper, salt, and pepper until the onions have softened.

Combine the garlic, lime juice, and egg white in a mixing dish.

Beat the egg yolks with an immersion blender

l they are light in color.

Continue to beat until it thickens into a sour cream texture.

Mix in the salt until it is well combined.

Put potatoes in a dish to eat.

Nutrition

Nutrition: Calories: 336, Carbs: 1 g Protein: 56 g Total Fat: 10 g

76. Vegetarian Spanish Toast with Escalivada

Preparation Time: 15 minutes

Cooking Time: 25 minutes

Servings: 3

Ingredients:

- Flat leaf parsley
- Sea salt to taste
- 80 g soft goat's cheese
- 1 slice Serrano ham
- ½ jar of Escalivada
- Green olives
- Extra virgin olive oil
- 1 large bruschetta bread

Directions

Directions:

After toasting one side of the bruschetta crust, sprinkle the uncooked side with olive oil.

Drain the escalivada with a fork.

Place the whole or doubled olives on top, then sprinkle the goat's cheese on top.

Put the toast back under the flame.

Blow the Spicy salami into small pieces and sprinkle them on top.

Cut into chunks or half and serve hot with a side dish of finely chopped flat leaf parsley and sea salt pinch.

Nutrition

Nutrition: Calories: 333, Carbs: 8.9 g Protein: 60.6 g Total Fat: 4.7 g

77. Vegetarian Garlic Soup with Egg and Croutons

Preparation Time: 15 minutes

Cooking Time: 25 minutes

Servings: 3

Ingredients:

- ¼ cup extra virgin olive oil
- Salt and pepper
- 1 tsp sweet paprika
- 1 liter chicken broth
- 2 eggs
- 6 garlic cloves
- 2 slices stale bread

Directions

Garlic should be peeled and cut into strips.

Heat the olive oil in a saucepan over medium heat.

Add garlic and cook for 23 minutes, or until it starts to brown.

Add the loaf to the pan and fry it with the garlic, allowing it to soak up the oil.

Reduce to low heat and stir in the parmesan.

Put in the liquid and give it a good swirl.

Take the soup to a rolling simmer, reduce to low heat, and continue cooking for about thirty minu-tes.

To taste, season with salt and pepper, using at least ½ teaspoon of pepper.

In a large mixing bowl, whisk together the eggs and add them to the soup.

Nutrition

Nutrition: Calories: 420, Carbs: 16 g Protein: 30 g Total Fat: 26 g

78. Mediterranean Baked Vegetarian Tapas

Preparation Time: 15 minutes

Cooking Time: 25 minutes

Servings: 3

Ingredients:

- 1 tbsp olive oil
- Fresh basil
- 1 red onion
- 1 dl mató cheese
- 1 bag dates
- 250 g small tomatoes
- 2 cloves garlic
- 2 tbsp mató cheese
- A handful walnuts
- 1 eggplant
- 1 tbsp maple syrup

Directions

Roll the dates and fill them with hazelnuts and Spanish Mató cheese.

Place on a tray and drizzle with maple syrup to finish.

Wash the tomatoes and cut them in half.

Parsley and red onion should be chopped.

Combine the tomato and Mató cheese in a mixing dish.

Wash the eggplant and break it into thin slices.

Steam for 23 minutes on each side after brushing with canola oil.

Cover them in foil and place them on a tray.

Place olive tapenade, polenta, cello, oranges, artichokes, Manchego cheese, heat tomatoes, fluffy biscuits, and Spanish wine on the tapas table.

Nutrition

Nutrition: Calories: 294, Carbs: 11 g Protein: 23.9 g Total Fat: 18.2 g

79. Vegetarian Pan con Tomate

Preparation Time: 15 minutes

Cooking Time: 25 minutes

Servings: 3

Ingredients:

- 2 medium cloves garlic
- Flaky sea salt
- 1 loaf ciabatta
- Extra virgin olive oil
- Kosher salt
- 2 large tomatoes

Directions

Tomatoes should be cut in half vertically. In a big mixing bowl, grate a box grinder.

Preheat the broiler to high and position the rack 4 inches below it.

Spoonful olive oil over the cut side of the bread on a work surface.

Use kosher salt, and season to taste.

Position the bread cutting side up on a rack set in a pan or immediately on the griddle rack and broil for 2 or 3 minutes, or until crispy and beginning to char form around the edge.

beginning to char form around the edge.

Take the bread from the microwave and scrub it with the garlic cloves that have been cut.

Spread the tomato mixture on top of the pizza.

Dress with flaky sesame oil and rain of extra virgin canola oil.

Nutrition

Nutrition: Calories: 251, Carbs: 1 g Protein: 34 g Total Fat: 12 g

Chapter 7. Dinner Recipes

80. Mushrooms Stuffed & Crab Paste

Preparation Time: 15 minutes

Cooking Time: 20 minutes

Servings: 15

Ingredients:

- 20 oz/566 g mushrooms
- (about 20 mushrooms)
- 2 tbsp parmesan cheese
- 1 tbsp parsley (fresh, chopped)
- Salt to taste
- For filling:
- 4 oz/100 g cream cheese
- 4 oz crab meat (chopped)
- 5 garlic cloves (minced)
- 1 tsp oregano
- ½ tsp paprika
- ½ tsp pepper & ¼ tsp salt

Directions

Preheat the oven to 400°F/200°C. Put parchment paper over the baking sheet.

Remove the stems from the mushrooms. Put the mushroom heads over the baking sheet (not too close to each other). Sprinkle with salt.

In a bowl, mix the filling ingredients. (There should be no lumps of cream cheese.) With a teas-poon, carefully stuff the mushroom caps with this cheese mix.

Sprinkle parmesan on top of each mushroom head.

Bake for half an hour or until the mushrooms are soft and the parmesan cheese is brownish.

Nutrition

Nutrition: Calories: 34.1, g Cholesterol: 4.7 mg Carbs: 2.7 g Protein: 5.0 g

81. Chicken Skewers with Peppers and Pineapple

Preparation Time: 15 minutes

Cooking Time: 20 minutes

Servings: 15

Ingredients:

- 600 g chicken breast
- 400 g peppers
- 320 g fresh or canned natural pineapple
- 3 tbsp extra virgin olive oil
- 4 garlic cloves
- 2 tsp lemon juice
- Salt to taste
- Kitchen skewers
-
- For the sauce:
- 400 ml sugar-free pineapple juice
- 4 tsp corn starch
- 4 tbsp tomato puree
- 4 tsp balsamic vinegar
- Chili pepper powder
- Salt to taste
- Pepper to taste

Directions

First, prepare the sauce, put all the ingredients in a saucepan, add the corn starch with a sieve and cook over low heat, stirring to prevent lumps from forming.

When the sauce is smooth, season with salt and pepper and turn off the heat. In the meantime, cut the chicken breast, peppers and pineapple into coarse cubes and alternate them on the skewers.

Prepare a marinade with crushed garlic, lemon juice, a pinch of salt and extra virgin olive oil. Let it flavor for a few minutes, brush the skewers and let them rest for 5-10 minutes.

Brown the skewers in a non-stick pan cover them and cook for 15 minutes, turning them on one side and the other to cook them well. Arrange the skewers on a platter, sail with the prepared sauce and serve them on the table. Chicken skewers with peppers and pineapple lend themselves to be eaten hot or cold.

Nutrition

Nutrition: Calories: 315, Fat: 20.9 g Protein: 15.8 g Carbs: 5.4 g Fiber: 0.4 g

82. Greek Salad Skewers

Preparation Time: 15 minutes

Cooking Time: 30 minutes

Servings: 2

Ingredients:

- 2 wooden sticks, absorbed water for 30 minutes before use
- 8 enormous dark olives
- 8 cherry tomatoes
- 1 yellow pepper, cut into 8 squares
- ½ red onion, cut down the middle and isolated into 8 pieces
- 100 g (about 10 cm) cucumber, cut into 4 cuts and divided
- 100 g feta, cut into 8 shapes
-
- For the dressing:
- 1 tbsp additional virgin olive oil
- ½ lemon, juiced
- 1 tsp balsamic vinegar
- ½ clove garlic, stripped and squashed
- Scarcely any departs basil, finely hacked (or ½ tsp dried blended herbs to supplant basil and oregano) leaves oregano, finely slashed
- Liberal flavoring of salt and crisply ground dark pepper

Directions

Thread each stick with the plate of mixed greens ingredients in the request: olive, tomato, yellow pepper, red onion, cucumber, feta, tomato, olive, yellow pepper, red onion, cucumber, and feta. Place all the dressing ingredients in a little bowl and combine them all. Pour over the sticks.

Nutrition

Nutrition: Calories: 364, Fat: 2 g Carbs: 12 g Protein: 12 g Fiber: 0 g

83. Sweet-Smelling Chicken Breast with Kale, Red Onion, and Salsa

Preparation Time: 15 minutes

Cooking Time: 35 minutes

Servings: 2

Ingredients:

- 120 g skinless, boneless chicken bosom
- 2 tsp ground turmeric
- ¼ lemon, juiced
- 1 tbsp additional virgin olive oil
- 50 g kale, slashed
- 20 g red onion, cut
- 1 tsp slashed new ginger
- 50 g buckwheat

Directions

To make the salsa, expel the eye from the tomato and slash it finely, taking consideration to keep however much of the fluid as could reasonably be expected.

Blend in with the bean stew, tricks, parsley, and lemon juice. You could place everything in a blender, yet the final product is somewhat different.

Warm the broiler to 220ºC/gas 7. Marinate the chicken bosom in 1 teaspoon of turmeric, lemon juice, and a little oil. Leave for 5–10 minutes.

Warmth an ovenproof griddle until hot, then include the marinated chicken and cook for a moment or so on each side, until pale brilliant, then exchange to the broiler (place on a preparing plate if your skillet isn't ovenproof) for 8–10 minutes or until cooked through.

Expel from the broiler, spread with foil, and leave to rest for 5 minutes before serving. In the meantime, cook the kale in a steamer for 5 minutes. Fry the red onions and the ginger in a little oil, until delicate but not shaded, then include the cooked kale and fry for one more moment.

Cook the buckwheat according to the parcel Directions with the rest of the teaspoon of turmeric. Serve nearby the chicken, vegetables, and salsa.

Nutrition

Nutrition: Calories: 465, Fat: 2 g Carbs: 12 g Protein: 12 g Fiber: 0 g

84. Tuscan Bean Stew

Preparation Time: 15 minutes

Cooking Time: 40 minutes

Servings: 1

Ingredients:

- 1 tbsp additional virgin olive oil
- 50 g red onion, finely hacked
- 30 g carrot, stripped and finely chopped
- 30 g celery, cut and finely hacked
- 1 garlic clove, finely hacked
- ½ 10,000-foot bean stew, finely slashed (discretionary)
- 1 tsp herbs de Provence
- 200 ml vegetable stock
- 1 x 400 g tin hacked Italian tomatoes
- 1 tsp tomato purée
- 200 g tinned blended beans
- 50 g kale, generally hacked
- 1 tbsp generally hacked parsley
- 40 g buckwheat

Directions

Spot the oil in a medium pot over a low-medium warmth and delicately fry the onion, carrot, celery, garlic, chili (if utilizing) and herbs, until the onion is delicate yet not shaded.

Include the stock, tomatoes and tomato purée and bring to the bubble. Include the beans and stew for 30 minutes.

Include the kale and cook for another 5–10 minutes, until delicate, then include the parsley. In the interim, cook the buckwheat according to the bundle directions, deplete, and afterward present it with the stew.

and afterward present it with the stew.

Nutrition: Calories: 289 Fat: 2 g Carbs: 10 g Protein: 12 g Fiber: 0 g

85. Fragrant Asian Hotpot

Preparation Time: 10 minutes

Cooking Time: 15 minutes

Servings: 2

Ingredients:

- 1 tsp tomato purée
- 1 star anise, squashed (or ¼ tsp ground anise)
- Little bunch (10 g) parsley, stalks finely cleaved
- Little bunch (10 g) coriander, stalks finely cleaved
- ½ lime, juiced
- 500 ml chicken stock, new or made with 1 solid shape
- ½ carrot, stripped and cut into matchsticks
- 50 g broccoli, cut into little florets
- 50 g beansprouts
- 100 g crude tiger prawns
- 100 g firm tofu, slashed
- 50 g rice noodles, cooked according to parcel directions
- 50 g cooked water chestnuts, depleted
- 20 g sushi ginger, slashed
- 1 tbsp great quality miso glue

Directions

Spot the tomato purée, star anise, parsley stalks, coriander stalks, lime juice and chicken stock in an enormous container and bring to a stew for 10 minutes.

Include the carrot, broccoli, prawns, tofu, noodles and water chestnuts, and stew tenderly until the prawns are cooked through.

Expel from the warmth and mix in the sushi ginger and miso glue. Serve sprinkled with parsley and coriander leaves.

Nutrition

Nutrition: Calories: 434, Fat: 2 g Carbs: 12 g Protein: 12 g Fiber: 0 g

86. Chicken Fry with Peanut Sauce

Preparation Time: 10 minutes

Cooking Time: 15 minutes

Servings: 4

Ingredients:

- Meat from 4 chicken thighs, cut into bite-size pieces
- 2 tbsp + ¼ cup peanut oil
- ½ cup peanut butter
- 3 tbsp toasted sesame oil
- 2 tbsp soy sauce
- 1 tbsp lime juice
- 1 clove garlic, minced
- 1 tsp powdered ginger

- 1-2 tsp hot sauce, if desired
- 2 red bell peppers, chopped
- 2 tbsp toasted sesame seeds
- 4 green onions, thinly sliced

Directions

Heat 2 tablespoons of peanut oil in a large frying pan.

Add the chicken and cook for about 10 minutes, until no pink remains.

Meanwhile, mix the peanut butter, ¼ cup peanut oil, sesame oil, soy sauce, lime juice, garlic, ginger, and hot sauce.

Add more water if needed to achieve a smooth consistency.

When the chicken is done, add the red pepper and cook for 1 minute more.

Divide the chicken and peppers between 4 plates and top with peanut sauce, toasted sesame seeds, and green onions.

Nutrition

Nutrition: Calories: 426.9, Sugars: 4.8 g Total Carbs: 16.9 g Protein: 38.7 g

87. Toasted Sardines with Parsley

Preparation Time: 10 minutes

Cooking Time: 15 minutes

Servings: 4

Ingredients:

- 400 g fresh sardines already cleaned
- 2 lemons zest
- Salt to taste
- 50 g chopped parsley
- 1 tsp black pepper
- 1 crushed clove garlic
- 2 tbsp white wine
- 1 tbsp extra-virgin olive oil

Directions

Prepare the sauce by blending the parsley, pepper, garlic clove and thinly grated lemon zest. Also add the white wine, lemon juice and oil.

Cook the sardines in a non-stick pan (or grill) for 1 minute per side.

When serving, pour a little sauce on the plate, lay the sardines on top, and season with other sauce. Complete with a pinch of salt and lemon zest cut into strips.

Nutrition

Nutrition: Calories: 300, Fat: 16.9 g Protein: 20.3 g Carbs: 6.9 g Fiber: 0.9 g

88. Savory Crêpes with Vegetables

Preparation Time: 5 minutes

Cooking Time: 15 minutes

Servings: 12

Ingredients:

- For The Crepes Batter:
- 2 eggs
- 90 g 00 flour
- 150 ml partially skimmed milk
- 1 pinch salt
- ½ tsp extra virgin olive oil
- For The Stuffing:
- 500 g spinach
- 10 g parmesan
- Salt to taste
- Pepper to taste
-
- For the dressing:
- 300 g cherry tomatoes
- 1 clove garlic
- 1 tsp extra virgin olive oil
- Salt to taste
- Basil leaves

Directions

Start preparing the crepes batter: beat the eggs in a bowl with the help of a whisk, add the milk, and a pinch of salt and beat again.

Add the sifted flour, little by little, stirring constantly with the whisk to create a smooth and homogeneous, lump-free batter.

Heat half a teaspoon of oil in a non-stick pan or a crepe pan, with a sheet of absorbent paper and remove the excess oil.

When it is hot, pour a ladle of batter and cook for about 2 minutes on low heat. Turn the crepes over and cook for 1-2 minutes. Repeat the operation until the batter runs out.

Boil the spinach in boiling water, when they are soft, drain, squeeze them and let them cool. Season them with salt, pepper and grated parmesan.

Prepare the dressing by heating the teaspoon of oil with the clove of garlic, split in 2 in a pan.

Add the previously cut cherry tomatoes, salt, and pepper and leave to boil for about 5 minutes.

Fill the crepes with the spinach filling, season with the sautéed cherry tomatoes, and serve with fresh basil leaves.

Nutrition

Nutrition: Calories: 150, Fat: 7 g Protein: 10.3 g Carbs: 5.4 g Fiber: 0.7 g

89. Fusilli Pasta with Cherry Tomatoes, Capers and Crunchy Crumbs

Preparation Time: 10 minutes

Cooking Time: 40 minutes

Servings: 4

Ingredients :

- Wholemeal bread
- Salted capers
- 1 clove garlic
- 1 hot pepper
- Oblong cherry tomatoes
- Extra virgin olive oil
- Salt to taste
- Fusilli

Directions

To make the fusilli with cherry tomatoes, capers and crunchy crumbs, start putting a pot of lightly salted water on the fire to boil the pasta. So, dedicate yourself to seasoning.

Chop the bread and put it in a hot pan together with the desalted capers, the clove of garlic and the chili pepper. Toast stirring often so that it is uniformly colored without burning.

Cut the cherry tomatoes in half and remove the seeds. Arrange them in a colander, add a pinch of salt and let them lose the excess vegetable water.

Remove the garlic clove and transfer the toast with the capers and the chili pepper into the mixer. Cut into crumbs.

Put everything back in a pan on high heat and give it one last toast to take a nice brown color, obviously without burning.

Heat 3 or 4 tablespoons of oil in a pan and add the cherry tomatoes that you will sauté for a few seconds over a high flame.

Drain the al dente fusilli, add them to the cherry tomatoes and sauté for a minute.

Divide into individual dishes, and finish with a generous sprinkling of bread, and a round of oil as desired

Nutrition

Nutrition: Calories: 210, Sodium: 23 mg Dietary Fiber: 6.4 g Total Fat: 2.1 g Total Carbs: 2.3 g Protein: 10.3 g

90. Pan-cooked Aubergine Olives and Capers

Preparation Time: 10 minutes

Cooking Time: 20 minutes

Servings: 4

Ingredients:

- 5 tomatoes
- 2 onions
- 2 cloves of garlic
- 1 tbsp pitted Taggiasca olives
- 1 tbsp salted capers
- A sprig parsley
- Extra virgin olive oil
- 1 tbsp vinegar
- 1 tsp sugar
- Salt to taste
- Black pepper to taste
- 4 small Aubergine

Directions

Wash and dry the eggplant

Cut them into cubes after removing the central part, which is particularly rich in seeds.

Leave them in salt for half an hour so that they will lose some of the bitter water.

After half an hour, rinse the Aubergine cubes and dry them. In a saucepan, heat 2 cups of chia of oil, add the onions, cut in icing and the whole cloves of garlic.

When they are slightly golden, remove the cloves of garlic and add the Aubergine cubes, then add the fresh tomatoes, seeded and diced: salt and pepper.

Cook over medium heat for about a quarter of an hour, stirring frequently so that eggplants and tomatoes do not stick to the bottom of the pan.

Now add the finely chopped parsley, olives, capers rinsed of salt and squeezed, vinegar and sugar.

Let it flavor well and then taste the Aubergine to check that they have a sweet and sour taste: if they were too sour, add a pinch of sugar, if they were too sweet add a splash of vinegar.

After a few minutes, remove from the heat: you can serve the eggplants in a pan with olives and warm or lukewarm capers.

Nutrition

Nutrition: Calories: 270, Sodium: 13 mg Dietary Fiber: 6.4 g Total Fat: 3.1 g Total Carbs: 213 g Protein: 10.3 g

91. Avocado Lime Shrimp Salad

Preparation Time: 15 minutes

Cooking Time: 0 minutes

Servings: 2

Ingredients:

- 14 oz jumbo cooked shrimp, peeled and deveined; chopped
- 4 ½ oz avocado, diced
- 1 ½ cup tomato, diced
- ¼ cup chopped green onion
- ¼ cup jalapeno with the seeds removed, diced fine
- 1 tsp olive oil
- 2 tbsp lime juice
- ⅛ tsp salt
- 1 tbsp chopped cilantro

Directions

Combine in a bowl: the green onion, olive oil, lime juice, pepper and a pinch of salt, now you will need to wait about 4 minutes until everything marinates and the onion becomes sweeter.

Get a large bowl and combined chopped shrimp, tomato, avocado, and jalapeno. Combine all of the ingredients, add cilantro, and gently toss.

Add pepper and salt as desired.

Nutrition: Calories: 314, Protein: 26 g Carbs: 15 g Fiber: 9 g

92. Rosemary Cauliflower Rolls

Preparation Time: 10 minutes

Cooking Time: 30 minutes

Servings: 3

Ingredients:

- ⅓ cup almond flour
- 4 cups riced cauliflower
- ⅓ cup reduced-fat, shredded mozzarella or cheddar cheese
- 2 eggs
- 2 tbsp fresh rosemary, finely chopped
- ½ tsp salt

Directions

Preheat your oven to 400°F

Combine all the listed ingredients in a medium-sized bowl

Scoop cauliflower mixture into 12 evenly-sized rolls/biscuits onto a lightly-greased and foil-lined baking sheet.

Bake until it turns golden brown, which should be achieved in about 30 minutes.

Note: if you want to have the outside of the rolls/biscuits crisp, then broil for some minutes before serving.

Nutrition

Nutrition: Calories: 254, Protein: 24 g Carbs: 7 g Fat: 8 g

93. Delicious Lemon Chicken Salad

Preparation Time: 15 minutes

Cooking Time: 5 minutes

Servings: 4

Ingredients:

- 1 lb chicken breast, cooked and diced
- 1 tbsp fresh dill, chopped
- 2 tsp olive oil
- ¼ cup low-fat yogurt
- 1 tsp lemon zest, grated
- 2 tbsp onion, minced
- ¼ tsp pepper
- ¼ tsp salt

Directions

Put all your fixing into the large mixing bowl and toss well. Season with pepper and salt. Cover and place in the refrigerator. Serve chilled and enjoy.

Nutrition

Nutrition: Calories: 165, Fat: 5.4 g Protein: 25.2 g Carbs: 2.2 g Sodium 153 mg

94. Healthy Chicken Orzo

Preparation Time: 15 minutes

Cooking Time: 15 minutes

Servings: 4

Ingredients:

- ½ tsp red pepper flakes
- ½ cup feta cheese, crumbled
- ½ tsp oregano
- 1 tbsp fresh parsley, chopped
- 1 tbsp fresh basil, chopped
- ¼ cup pine nuts
- 1 cup spinach, chopped
- ¼ cup white wine
- ½ cup olives, sliced
- 1 cup grape tomatoes, cut in half
- ½ tbsp garlic, minced
- 2 tbsp olive oil
- ½ tsp pepper
- ½ tsp salt
- 1 cup whole wheat orzo
- 1 lb chicken breasts, sliced
-

Directions

Add water to a small saucepan and bring to boil. Heat 1 tablespoon of olive oil in a pan over medium heat. Season chicken with pepper and salt and cook in the pan for 5-7 minutes on each side. Remove from pan and set aside.

Add orzo in boiling water and cook according to the packet directions. Heat the remaining olive oil in a pan on medium heat, then put garlic in the pan and sauté for a minute. Stir in white wine and cherry tomatoes and cook on high for 3 minutes.

Add cooked orzo, spices, spinach, pine nuts, and olives and stir until well combined. Add chicken on top of the orzo and sprinkle with feta cheese. Serve and enjoy.

Nutrition

Nutrition: Calories: 518, Fat: 27.7 g Protein: 40.6 g Carbs: 26.2 g Sodium 121 mg

95. Lemon Garlic Chicken

Preparation Time: 15 minutes

Cooking Time: 12 minutes

Servings: 3

Ingredients:

- 3 chicken breasts, cut into thin slices
- 2 lemon zest, grated
- ¼ cup olive oil
- 4 garlic cloves, minced
- Pepper to taste
- Salt taste

Directions

Warm-up olive oil in a pan over medium heat. Add garlic to the pan and sauté for 30 seconds. Put the chicken in the pan and sauté within 10 minutes. Add lemon zest and lemon juice and bring to boil. Remove from heat and season with pepper and salt. Serve and enjoy.

Nutrition

Nutrition: Calories: 439, Fat: 27.8 g Protein: 42.9 g Carbs: 4.9 g Sodium 306 mg

96. Chicken Cacciatore

Preparation Time: 5 minutes

Cooking Time: 45 minutes

Servings: 6

Ingredients:

- 2 tbsp extra virgin olive oil
- 6 chicken thighs
- 1 sweet onion, chopped
- 2 garlic cloves, minced
- 2 red bell peppers, cored and diced
- 2 carrots, diced
- 1 rosemary sprig
- 1 thyme sprig
- 4 tomatoes, peeled and diced
- ½ cup tomato juice
- ¼ cup dry white wine
- 1 cup chicken stock
- 1 bay leaf
- Salt and pepper to taste

Directions

Heat the oil in a heavy saucepan.

Cook chicken on all sides until golden.

Stir in the onion and garlic and cook for 2 minutes.

Stir in the rest of the ingredients and season with salt and pepper.

Cook on low heat for 30 minutes.

Serve the chicken cacciatore warm and fresh.

Nutrition

Nutrition: Calories: 363, Fat: 14 g Protein: 42 g Carbs: 9 g

97. Fennel Wild Rice Risotto

Preparation Time: 5 minutes

Cooking Time: 35 minutes

Servings: 6

Ingredients:

- 2 tbsp extra virgin olive oil
- 1 shallot, chopped
- 2 garlic cloves, minced
- 1 fennel bulb, chopped
- 1 cup wild rice
- ¼ cup dry white wine
- 2 cups chicken stock
- 1 tsp grated orange zest
- Salt and pepper to taste

 **Directions**

Heat the oil in a heavy saucepan.

Add the garlic, shallot and fennel and cook for a few minutes until softened.

Stir in the rice and cook for 2 additional minutes then add the wine, stock and orange zest, with salt and pepper to taste.

Cook on low heat for 20 minutes.

Serve the risotto warm and fresh.

 **Nutrition**

Nutrition: Calories: 162, Fat: 2 g Protein: 8 g Carbs: 20 g

98. Wild Rice Prawn Salad

Preparation Time: 5 minutes

Cooking Time: 35 minutes

Servings: 6

Ingredients:

- ¾ cup wild rice
- 1 ¾ cup chicken stock
- 1 lb prawns
- Salt and pepper to taste
- 2 tbsp lemon juice
- 2 tbsp extra virgin olive oil
- 2 cups arugula

 **Directions**

Combine the rice and chicken stock in a saucepan and cook until the liquid has been absorbed entirely.

Transfer the rice to a salad bowl.

Season the prawns with salt and pepper and drizzle them with lemon juice and oil.

Heat a grill pan over medium flame.

Place the prawns on the hot pan and cook on each side for 2-3 minutes.

For the salad, combine the rice with arugula and prawns and mix well.

Serve the salad fresh.

 **Nutrition**

Nutrition: Calories: 207, Fat: 4 g Protein: 20.6 g Carbs: 17 g

99. King Prawn Stir-fry & Soba

Preparation Time: 10 minutes

Cooking Time: 25 minutes

Servings: 2

Ingredients:

- 150 g shelled raw king prawns, deveined
- 2 tsp tamari
- 2 tsp extra virgin olive oil
- 75 soba
- 1 garlic clove, finely chopped

- 1 bird's eye chili, finely chopped
- 1 tsp finely chopped fresh ginger
- 20 g red onions, sliced
- 40 g celery, trimmed and sliced
- 75 g green beans, chopped

Directions

Warm a skillet over high heat, and then fry the pawns in 1 tsp of the tamari and 1 tsp of olive oil.

Transfer the contents of the skillet to a plate, and then wipe the skillet with a kitchen towel to remove the lingering sauce.

Boil water and cook the soba for 8 minutes, or according to packet directions.

Drain and set aside for later. Using the remaining 1 tsp olive oil, fry the remaining ingredients for 3-4 minutes. Add the stock and bring to a boil, simmering until the vegetables are tender but still have a bite.

Add the lovage, noodles, and prawn into the skillet, stir, bring back to a boil and then serve.

Nutrition

Nutrition: Calories: 435, Fat: 2 g Carbs: 12 g Protein: 12 g Fiber: 0 g

100. Baked Potatoes with Spicy Chickpea Stew

Preparation Time: 10 minutes

Cooking Time: 1 hour

Servings: 4-6

Ingredients:

- 4-6 baking potatoes, pricked around
- 2 tbsp olive oil
- 2 red onions, finely chopped
- 4 tsp garlic, crushed or grated
- 2 cm ginger, grated
- ½ -2 tsp chili flakes (depending on how hot you enjoy matters)
- 2 tbsp cumin seeds
- 2 tbsp turmeric
- Splash water
- 2 x 400 g tins chopped tomatoes
- 2 tbsp unsweetened cocoa powder (or even cacao)
- 2 x 400 g tins chickpeas (or kidney beans if you want) such as the chickpea water DON'T DRAIN!!
- 2 yellow peppers (or whatever color you would like!), chopped into bite-size pieces
- 2 tbsp parsley and additional garnish
- Salt and pepper to taste (optional)
- Side salad (optional)

Directions

Preheat the oven to 200°C; however, you can prepare all of your ingredients.

After the oven is warm enough place your baking potatoes from the oven and cook for 1 hour or so till they're done the way you like them.

When the potatoes are from the oven, set the olive oil and sliced red onion into a large wide saucepan and cook lightly, using the lid for 5 minutes until the onions are tender but not brown.

Remove the lid and add the ginger, garlic, and cumin and simmer. Cook for a further minute on very low heat, and then add the garlic and a tiny dab of water and then cook for one more moment just take care to not allow the pan to get too thick.

Then add the berries, cocoa powder (or even cacao), chickpeas (such as chickpea water) and salt. Bring to a boil, and then simmer on very low heat for 45 seconds before the sauce is thick and unctuous (but do not let it burn). The stew should be performed at approximately the same period as the legumes.

Finally, stir in the 2 tablespoons of parsley, and some pepper and salt if you desire, and also serve the stew in addition to the chopped potatoes, possibly with a very simple salad.

Nutrition

Nutrition: Calories: 213, Fat: 13.1 g Protein: 80.62 g Sugar: 51.67 g

101. Kale and Red Onion Dhal with Buckwheat

Preparation Time: 5 minutes

Cooking Time: 25 minutes

Servings: 4

Ingredients:

- 1 tbsp olive oil
- 1 small red onion, sliced
- 3 garlic cloves, crushed or grated
- 2 cm ginger, grated
- 1 bird's eye chili deseeded and finely chopped (more if you like things sexy!)
- 2 tsp turmeric
- 2 tsp gram masala
- 160 g red peas
- 400 ml coconut milk
- 200 ml water
- 100 g lettuce
- 160 g buckwheat (or brown rice)

Directions

Place the olive oil into a large, deep skillet and then add the chopped onion. Cook on, with the lid for 5 minutes until softened.

Add the ginger, garlic and chili, and cook for 1 minute.

Add the garlic, and gram masala along with a dash of water, and then cook for 1 minute.

Insert the red peas, almond milk, also 200ml water (do so by simply half-filling the coconut milk can with water and then tipping it into the saucepan).

Mix everything thoroughly and then cooks for 20 minutes over a gentle heat with the lid. Stir occasionally and add a bit more water if the dhal begins to stick.

After 20 minutes add the carrot, stir thoroughly and then replace the lid, then cook for a further 5 minutes (1-2 minutes if you use spinach)

Approximately 15 minutes before the curry is prepared, set the buckwheat into a medium saucepan and then put in lots of warm water. Bring back the water to a boil and cook for 10 minutes (or even a bit longer if you want your buckwheat softer. Drain the buckwheat at a sieve and function together with all the dhal.

Nutrition

Nutrition: Calories: 213, Fat: 13.1 g Protein: 80.62 g Sugar: 51.67 g

102. Date and Walnut Cinnamon Bites

Preparation Time: 10 minutes

Cooking Time: 5 minutes

Servings: 1

Ingredients:

- 3 walnut parts
- 3 pitted Medjool dates
- The ground cinnamon, to taste

Directions

Deliberately cut every walnut half into 3 cuts, at that point do likewise with the dates. Spot a cut of walnut on each date, dust with cinnamon and serve.

Nutrition

Nutrition: Calories: 100, Fat: 15 g Carbs: 35 g Protein: 1 g

103. Chicken Casserole

Preparation Time: 15 minutes

Cooking Time: 40 minutes

Servings: 4

Ingredients:

- 1 lb cooked chicken, shredded
- ¼ cup Greek yogurt
- 1 cup cheddar cheese, shredded
- ½ cup salsa
- 4 oz cream cheese, softened
- 4 cups cauliflower florets
- ⅛ tsp black pepper
- ½ tsp kosher salt

Directions

Add cauliflower florets to the microwave-safe dish and cook for 10 minutes or until tender.

Add cream cheese and microwave for 30 seconds more. Stir well.

Add the chicken, yogurt, cheddar cheese, sauce, pepper and salt and mix for a few minutes

Preheat oven to 370°F.

Bake in the preheated oven for 25 minutes.

Serve hot and enjoy.

Nutrition

Nutrition: Calories: 429, Fat: 23 g Carbs: 6 g Sugar 7 g Protein: 44 g Cholesterol: 149 mg

Chapter 8. Vegetables

104. Parsley Zucchini and Radishes

Preparation Time: 5 minutes

Cooking Time: 15 minutes

Servings: 4

Ingredients:

- 1 lb zucchinis, cubed
- 1 cup radishes, halved
- 1 tbsp olive oil
- 1 tbsp balsamic vinegar
- 2 tomatoes, cubed
- 3 tbsp parsley, chopped
- Salt and black pepper to the taste

Directions

In a pan that fits your air fryer, mix the zucchinis with the radishes, oil and the other ingredients, toss, introduce in the fryer and cook at 350°F for 15 minutes.

Divide between plates and serve as a side dish.

Nutrition

Nutrition: Calories: 170, Fat: 6 g Fiber: 2 g Carbs: 5 g Protein: 6 g

105. Cherry Tomatoes Sauté

Preparation Time: 5 minutes

Cooking Time: 15 minutes

Servings: 4

Ingredients:

- 1 tbsp olive oil
- 1 lb cherry tomatoes, halved
- 1 lime, juiced
- 2 tbsp parsley, chopped
- A pinch salt and black pepper

Directions

In a pan that fits the air fryer, mix the tomatoes with the oil and the other ingredients, toss, introduce the pan to the machine and cook at 360°F for 15 minutes.

Divide between plates and serve.

Nutrition

Nutrition: Calories: 141, Fat: 6 g Fiber: 2 g Carbs: 4 g Protein: 7 g

106. Creamy Eggplant

Preparation Time: 5 minutes

Cooking Time: 20 minutes

Servings: 4

Ingredients:

- 2 lb eggplants, roughly cubed
- 1 cup heavy cream
- Salt and black pepper to the taste
- ½ tsp chili powder
- ½ tsp turmeric powder

Directions

In a pan that fits the air fryer, mix the eggplants with the cream, and the other ingredients, toss, introduce in the machine and cook at 370°F for 20 minutes.

Divide between plates and serve as a side dish.

Nutrition

Nutrition: Calories: 151, Fat: 3 g Fiber: 2 g Carbs: 4 g Protein: 6 g

107. Eggplant and Carrots Mix

Preparation Time: 5 minutes

Cooking Time: 25 minutes

Servings: 4

Ingredients:

- 1 lb eggplants, roughly cubed
- 1 lb baby carrots
- 1 cup heavy cream
- ½ tsp chili powder
- 1 tsp garlic powder
- 1 tbsp chives, chopped
- A pinch salt and black pepper

Directions

In a pan that fits your air fryer, mix the eggplants with the carrots, cream and the other ingredients, toss, introduce in the air fryer and cook at 370°F for 25 minutes.

Divide between plates and serve as a side dish.

Nutrition

Nutrition: Calories: 129, Fat: 6 g Fiber: 2 g Carbs: 5 g Protein: 8 g

108. Parmesan Eggplants

Preparation Time: 5 minutes

Cooking Time: 20 minutes

Servings: 4

Ingredients:

- 1 lb eggplants, roughly cubed
- 1 tbsp olive oil
- 1 tsp garlic powder
- 1 cup parmesan, grated
- A pinch salt and black pepper
- Cooking spray

Directions

In the air fryer's pan, mix the eggplants with the oil and the other ingredients except for the parmesan and toss.

Sprinkle the parmesan on top, put the pan in the machine, and cook at 370°F for 20 minutes.

Divide between plates and serve as a side dish.

Nutrition

Nutrition: Calories: 183, Fat: 6 g Fiber: 2 g Carbs: 3 g Protein: 8 g

109. Kale Sauté

Preparation Time: 5 minutes

Cooking Time: 15 minutes

Servings: 4

Ingredients:

- 1 tbsp avocado oil
- 1 lb baby kale
- ½ cup heavy cream
- Salt and black pepper to the taste
- ¼ tsp chili powder
- 1 tbsp dill, chopped
- ¼ cup walnuts, chopped

Directions

In a pan that fits the air fryer, mix the kale with the oil, cream and the other ingredients, toss, introduce the pan to the machine and cook at 360°F for 15 minutes.

Divide between plates and serve as a side dish.

Nutrition

Nutrition: Calories: 160, Fat: 7g, Fiber: 2 g Carbs: 4 g Protein: 5 g

110. Carrots Sauté

Preparation Time: 5 minutes

Cooking Time: 20 minutes

Servings: 4

Ingredients:

- 2 lb baby carrots, peeled
- 1 tbsp balsamic vinegar
- 2 tbsp olive oil

- Salt and black pepper to the taste
- 1 tbsp lemon juice
- ⅓ cup almonds, chopped
- ½ cup walnuts, chopped

Directions

In a pan that fits the air fryer, mix the carrots with the vinegar, oil and the other ingredients, toss, introduce the pan to the machine and cook at 380°F for 20 minutes.

Divide between plates and serve as a side dish.

Nutrition

Nutrition: Calories: 121, Fat: 9 g Fiber: 2 g Carbs: 4 g Protein: 5 g

111. Bok Choy and Sprouts

Preparation Time: 5 minutes

Cooking Time: 20 minutes

Servings: 4

Ingredients:

- 1 tbsp avocado oil
- 1 lb Brussels sprouts, trimmed and halved
- 2 bok choy heads, trimmed and cut into strips
- 1 tbsp balsamic vinegar
- A pinch salt and black pepper
- 1 tbsp dill, chopped

Directions

In a pan that fits your air fryer, mix the sprouts with the bok choy and the other ingredients, toss, introduce the pan to the air fryer and cook at 380°F for 20 minutes.

Divide between plates and serve as a side dish.

Nutrition

Nutrition: Calories: 141, Fat: 3 g Fiber: 2 g Carbs: 4 g Protein: 3 g

112. Balsamic Radishes

Preparation Time: 10 minutes

Cooking Time: 20 minutes

Servings: 4

Ingredients:

- 1 lb radishes, halved
- 1 tbsp balsamic vinegar
- 1 tsp chili powder
- 1 tbsp avocado oil
- Salt and black pepper to the taste

Directions

In a pan that fits the air fryer, combine the radishes with the vinegar and the other ingredients, toss, introduce the pan to the air fryer and cook at 380°F for 20 minutes.

Divide between plates and serve as a side dish.

Nutrition: Calories: 151, Fat: 2 g Fiber: 3 g Carbs: 5 g Protein: 5 g

113. Spaghetti Squash Casserole

Preparation Time: 10 minutes

Cooking Time: 20 minutes

Servings: 4

Ingredients:

- 12 oz spaghetti squash
- 1 tsp ground cinnamon
- ½ tsp salt
- 1 sweet potato, grated
- 1 tbsp almond flour
- 2 eggs
- 1 tbsp olive oil
- 1 onion, diced
- ¼ tsp thyme

Directions

Peel the spaghetti squash and chop it into the ½ inch chunks.

Then place the squash in the air fryer basket.

Add salt and ground cinnamon.

Cook the sweet potatoes for 5 minutes at 380 F.

After this, make the layer of the grated potato over the sweet potato.

Beat the eggs in the bowl and whisk them.

Add almond flour and stir the mixture.

Then add olive oil, diced onion, and thyme.

Stir the mixture. Pour it over the grated potato.

Cook the casserole for 15 minutes at 365°F.

When the time is over and the casserole is cooked – let it chill a little and serve!

Nutrition: Calories: 166, Fat: 9.8 g Fiber: 2.6 g Carbs: 16.5 g Protein: 5.7 g

114. Cinnamon Baby Carrot

Preparation Time: 8 minutes

Cooking Time: 15 minutes

Servings: 4

Ingredients:

- 1 lb baby carrot
- 1 tbsp ground cinnamon
- 1 tsp ground ginger
- ¼ cup almond milk
- 1 tbsp olive oil

Directions

Wash the baby carrot carefully and sprinkle it with ground cinnamon, ground ginger, and olive oil.

Stir the vegetables and transfer them to the air fryer basket.

Cook the baby carrot for 10 minutes at 380°F.

Then stir the baby carrots and add almond milk.

Stir the vegetables again and cook for 5 minutes more at the same temperature.

Let the cooked carrot chill a little and serve it!

Nutrition

Nutrition: Calories: 110, Fat: 7.3 g Fiber: 4.6 g Carbs: 11.9 g Protein: 1.2 g

115. Eggplant Tongues

Preparation Time: 10 minutes

Cooking Time: 14 minutes

Servings: 2

Ingredients:

- 2 eggplants
- 1 tsp minced garlic
- 1 tsp olive oil
- ¼ tsp ground black pepper

Directions

Wash the eggplants carefully and slice them.

Rub every eggplant slice with the minced garlic, olive oil, and ground black pepper.

Place the eggplants in the air fryer basket and cook for 7 minutes from each side at 375 F.

When the eggplant tongues are cooked – serve them immediately!

Nutrition

Nutrition: Calories: 160, Fat: 3.3 g Fiber: 19.4 g Carbs: 32.9 g Protein: 5.5 g

116. Super Tasty red Onion Petals

Preparation Time: 10 minutes

Cooking Time: 15 minutes

Servings: 4

Ingredients:

- 13 oz red onion, peeled
- 1 tsp basil, dried
- 1 tsp ground coriander
- 1 tbsp olive oil
- ¼ tsp ground nutmeg
- ¾ tsp turmeric

Directions

Cut the onion into the petals and sprinkle with the basil, ground coriander, olive oil, ground nutmeg, and turmeric.

Mix the onion petals and transfer them to the air fryer basket.

Cook the petals for 15 minutes at 375 F. Stir the petals every 3 minutes.

When the onion petals are cooked – they will have a soft texture.

Serve the side dish immediately!

Nutrition

Nutrition: Calories: 69, Fat: 3.7 g Fiber: 2.1 g Carbs: 9 g Protein: 1 g

117. Eggplant Garlic Salad with Tomatoes

Preparation Time: 10 minutes

Cooking Time: 15 minutes

Servings: 6

Ingredients:

- 3 tomatoes, chopped
- 2 eggplants, chopped
- 1 tbsp olive oil
- 1 tsp avocado oil
- 1 tbsp vinegar
- ½ tsp ground black pepper
- ½ tsp dried basil
- ½ tsp dried basil
- 2 garlic cloves, chopped

Directions

Place the chopped eggplants in the air fryer.

Sprinkle the eggplants with olive oil, ground black pepper, and dried basil.

Stir the eggplants and cook for 15 minutes at 390°F. Stir the vegetables every 5 minutes.

Then place the tomatoes in the bowl.

Add cooked eggplants, vinegar, and chopped garlic.

Then sprinkle the salad with the avocado oil and stir it.

Serve the cooked salad or keep it in the fridge!

Nutrition

Nutrition: Calories: 80, Fat: 2.9 g Fiber: 7.3 g Carbs: 13.6 g Protein: 2.4 g

118. Curry Eggplants

Preparation Time: 10 minutes

Cooking Time: 14 minutes

Servings: 2

Ingredients:

- 2 eggplants
- 1 tsp vinegar

- 1 tbsp olive oil
- 1 tsp curry powder
- 1 garlic clove
- 3 tbsp chicken stock

Directions

Peel the eggplants and cut them into cubes.

Sprinkle the eggplants with the curry powder and chicken stock.

Put the vegetables in the air fryer and cook for 14 minutes at 390°F.

Stir the eggplants every 5 minutes.

When the eggplants are cooked – let them chill till room temperature.

Sprinkle the vegetables with olive oil and vinegar. Stir and serve!

Nutrition

Nutrition: Calories: 204, Fat: 8.2 g Fiber: 19.7 g Carbs: 33.4 g Protein: 5.7 g

119. Sauteed Asparagus

Preparation Time: 10 minutes

Cooking Time: 8 minutes

Servings: 2

Ingredients:

- 1 onion, chopped
- ½ lemon
- 14 oz asparagus
- 2 tsp myrtle
- 1 tsp salt

Directions

Place the onion, salt, and myrtle in the air fryer basket.

Cook it at 400°F for 2 minutes.

Meanwhile, chop the asparagus roughly.

Place the chopped asparagus in the air fryer basket.

Squeeze the lemon juice over the asparagus and stir it.

Cook the side dish for 6 minutes at 395°F. Stir it every 3 minutes of cooking.

Let the cooked asparagus chill a little.

Enjoy!

Nutrition

Nutrition: Calories: 86, Fat: 2.5 g Fiber: 5.9 g Carbs: 14.8 g Protein: 5.2 g

120. Fennel Slices

Preparation Time: 10 minutes

Cooking Time: 10 minutes

Servings: 2

Ingredients:

- 12 oz fennel bulb
- 1 tsp paprika
- ½ tsp chili flakes
- 1 tbsp olive oil
- 1 tsp cilantro, dried

 **Directions**

Slice the fennel bulb and sprinkle it with the paprika, chili flakes, and dried cilantro on each side.

Then sprinkle the fennel with the olive oil and transfer the vegetables to the air fryer basket.

Cook the fennel slices for 10 minutes at 380 F. Flip the fennel slices into another side after 5 minutes of cooking.

Enjoy the cooked side dish!

 **Nutrition**

Nutrition: Calories: 116, Fat: 7.5 g Fiber: 5.7 g Carbs: 13 g Protein: 2.3 g

121. Butternut Squash Rice

Preparation Time: 10 minutes

Cooking Time: 20 minutes

Servings: 4

Ingredients:

- 1 lb butternut squash
- 1 tbsp myrtle
- 1 onion, diced
- 1 tsp salt
- 1 oz fresh parsley, chopped
- 1 tbsp olive oil

 **Directions**

Chop the butternut squash into the rice pieces.

Put the myrtle in the air fryer basket and add diced onion.

Sprinkle the onion with salt and olive oil.

Cook it at 400°F for 2 minutes.

Then stir the onion and add the butternut squash rice.

Stir it and cook the meal for 18 minutes at 380 F.

Stir the squash every 4 minutes.

When the meal is cooked – sprinkle it with the chopped parsley and stir.

Serve it immediately!

Nutrition: Calories: 123, Fat: 6.9 g Fiber: 3.1 g Carbs: 16.3 g Protein: 1.7 g

122. Eggplant Lasagna

Preparation Time: 20 minutes

Cooking Time: 30 minutes

Servings: 3

Ingredients:

- 1 eggplant
- 2 tomatoes
- 1 tbsp olive oil
- 1 onion, diced
- 1 garlic clove, chopped
- 1 tsp dried basil
- 1 tsp ground black pepper
- ½ tsp turmeric
- 1 tsp cumin
- ½ cup chicken stock
- 1 tbsp fresh dill, chopped
- 4 oz mushrooms, chopped

Directions

Slice the eggplants. Slice the tomatoes.

Combine the diced onion, olive oil, chopped garlic, dried basil, ground black pepper, turmeric, cumin, and fresh dill in the bowl.

Stir the mixture. Then make the layer of the sliced eggplants in the air fryer basket.

Sprinkle it with the spice mixture. Put the tomatoes over the eggplants and add mushrooms.

Sprinkle the vegetables with the spice mixture and repeat all the steps till you finish all the ingredients. Add chicken stock and cook lasagna for 30 minutes at 365°F.

Let the cooked lasagna chill a little and serve it!

Nutrition

Nutrition: Calories: 127, Fat: 5.6 g Fiber: 8 g Carbs: 18.9 g Protein: 4.4 g

123. Stuffed Eggplants with Cherry Tomatoes

Preparation Time: 15 minutes

Cooking Time: 25 minutes

Servings: 2

Ingredients:

- 1 eggplant
- 5 oz cherry tomatoes
- 1 shallot, chopped
- ½ tsp salt
- ¾ tsp nutmeg
- ¾ tsp chili pepper
- 1 tbsp olive oil

Directions

Cut the eggplant into halves.

Remove the meat from the eggplants.

Chop the cherry tomatoes and combine them with the salt, shallot, nutmeg, chili pepper, and olive oil.

Stir the mixture.

Fill the eggplants with vegetables.

Put the stuffed vegetables in the air fryer basket and cook for 25 minutes at 370 F.

Then chill the cooked eggplants a little.

Serve!

Nutrition

Nutrition: Calories: 136, Fat: 7.9 g Fiber: 9.2 g Carbs: 16.9 g Protein: 3 g

Chapter 9. Salads

124. Satisfying Spring Salad

Preparation Time: 5 minutes

Cooking Time: 10 minutes

Servings: 2

Ingredients:

- 4 oz arugula
- ½ cup cherry tomatoes halved
- ¼ cup basil leaves
- ½ key lime, juiced
- 2 tbsp walnuts
-
- Extra:
- ¼ tsp salt
- ⅛ tsp cayenne pepper

Directions

Prepare the dressing and for this, take a small bowl, place key lime juice in it, add salt, and cayenne pepper and then whisk until combined.

Take a medium bowl, place arugula, tomatoes, and basil leaves in it, pour in the dressing and then massage using your hands.

Let the salad rest for 20 minutes, then taste to adjust seasoning and then serve.

Nutrition

Nutrition: Calories: 87.3, Fat: 7 g Protein: 1.4 g Carbs: 6 g Fiber: 1.3 g

125. The Raw Green Detox Salad

Preparation Time: 5 minutes

Cooking Time: 0 minutes

Servings: 2

Ingredients:

- ½ cucumber, deseeded
- 4 oz arugula
- ⅛ tsp salt
- 1 tbsp key lime juice
- 1 tbsp olive oil
- Extra:
- ⅛ tsp cayenne pepper

Directions

Cut the cucumber into slices, add to a salad bowl, and then add arugula in it.

Mix lime juice and oil until combined, pour over the salad, and then season with salt and cayenne pepper.

Toss until mixed and then serve.

Nutrition

Nutrition: Calories: 142, Fat: 12.5 g Protein: 1.6 g Carbs: 7.8 g Fiber: 1 g

126. Dandelion Salad

Preparation Time: 10 minutes

Cooking Time: 7 minutes

Servings: 2

Ingredients:

- ½ onion, peeled, sliced
- 5 strawberries, sliced
- 2 cups dandelion greens, rinsed
- 1 tbsp key lime juice
- 1 tbsp grapeseed oil
-
- Extra:
- ¼ tsp salt

Directions

Take a medium skillet pan, place it over medium heat, add oil and let it heat until warm.

Add onion, season with ⅛ teaspoon salt, stir until mixed and then cook for 3 to 5 minutes until tender and golden brown.

Meanwhile, take a small bowl, place slices of strawberries in it, drizzle with ½ tablespoon lime juice and then toss until coated.

When onions have turned golden brown, stir in remaining lime juice, stir until mixed, and then cook for 1 minute.

Remove pan from heat, transfer onions into a large salad bowl, add strawberries and juices and dandelion greens, and then sprinkle with the remaining salt. Toss until mixed and then serve.

Nutrition

Nutrition: Calories: 204, Fat: 16.1 g Protein: 7 g Carbs: 10.6 g Fiber: 2.8 g

127. Spicy Wakame Salad

Preparation Time: 15 minutes

Cooking Time: 0 minutes

Servings: 2

Ingredients:

- 1 cup wakame stems
- ½ tbsp chopped red bell pepper
- ½ tsp onion powder
- ½ tbsp key lime juice
- Extra:
- ½ tbsp agave syrup
- ½ tbsp sesame seeds
- ½ tbsp sesame oil

 **Directions**

Place wakame stems in a bowl, cover with water, let them soak for 10 minutes, and then drain.

Meanwhile, prepare the dressing for this, take a small bowl, add lime juice, onion, agave syrup, and sesame oil in it and then whisk until blended.

Place drained wakame stems in a large dish, add bell pepper, pour in the dressing, and then toss until coated.

Sprinkle sesame seeds over the salad and then serve.

 **Nutrition**

Nutrition: Calories: 106, Fat: 7.3 g Protein: 3 g Carbs: 8 g Fiber: 1.7 g

128. Avo-Orange Salad Dish

Preparation Time: 5 minutes

Cooking Time: 0 minutes

Servings: 2

Ingredients:
- 1 orange, peeled, sliced
- 4 cups greens
- ½ avocado, peeled, pitted, and diced
- 2 tbsp slivered red onion
- ½ cup cilantro
- Extra:
- ¼ tsp salt
- ¼ cup olive oil
- 2 tbsp lime juice
- 2 tbsp orange juice

 **Directions**

Prepare the dressing and for this, place cilantro in a food processor, pour in orange juice, lime juice, and oil, add salt and then pulse until blended.

Tip the dressing into a mason jar. Add remaining ingredients, toss until coated, add to a salad bowl, or serve in the jar.

Nutrition: Calories: 106, Fat: 7.3 g Protein: 3 g Carbs: 8 g Fiber: 1.7 g

129. Nourishing Electric Salad

Preparation Time: 5 minutes

Cooking Time: 0 minutes

Servings: 2

Ingredients:

- ½ medium cucumber, deseeded, chopped
- 6 leaves of lettuce, broken into pieces
- 4 mushrooms, chopped
- 6 cherry tomatoes, chopped
- 10 olives
-
- Extra:
- ½ lime, juiced
- 1 tsp olive oil
- ¼ tsp salt

Directions

Take a medium salad bowl, place all the ingredients in it and then toss until mixed.

Nutrition: Calories: 129, Fat: 7 g Protein: 2 g Carbs: 14 g Fiber: 4 g

130. Superfood Fonio Salad

Preparation Time: 10 minutes

Cooking Time: 5 minutes

Servings: 2

Ingredients:

- ½ cup cooked chickpeas
- ¼ cup chopped cucumber
- ½ cup chopped red pepper
- ½ cup cherry tomatoes halved
- ½ cup fonio
-
- Extra:
- ⅓ tsp salt
- 1 tbsp grapeseed oil
- ⅛ tsp cayenne pepper
- 1 key lime, juiced
- 1 cup spring water

Directions

Take a medium saucepan, place it over high heat, pour in water, and bring it to boil.

Add fonio, switch heat to the low level, cook for 1 minute, and then remove the pan from heat.

Cover the pan with its lid, let fonio rest for 5 minutes, fluff by using a fork, and then let it cool for 15 minutes.

Take a salad bowl, place lime juice and oil in it and then stir in salt and cayenne pepper until combined.

Add remaining ingredients including fonio, toss until mixed, and then serve.

Nutrition

Nutrition: Calories: 145, Fat: 3 g Protein: 6 g Carbs: 24.5 g Fiber: 5.5 g

131. Healthy Chickpea Roast Salad

Preparation Time: 10 minutes

Cooking Time: 20 minutes

Servings: 2

Ingredients:

- ½ cucumber, deseeded, sliced
- 2 avocados, peeled, pitted, cubed
- 1 medium white onion, peeled, diced
- 2 cups cooked chickpeas
- ¼ cup chopped coriander
-
- Extra:
- 1 tsp onion powder
- ½ tsp cayenne pepper
- 1 tsp sea salt
- 2 tbsp hemp seeds, shelled
- 1 key lime, juiced
- 1 tbsp olive oil

Directions

Switch on the oven, then set it to 425°F and let it preheat.

Meanwhile, take a baking sheet, place chickpeas on it, season with salt, onion powder, and pepper, drizzle with oil and then toss until combined.

Bake the chickpeas for 20 minutes or until golden brown and crisp, then let them cool for 10 minutes.

Transfer chickpeas to a bowl, add remaining ingredients and stir until combined.

Nutrition

Nutrition: Calories: 208.3, Fat: 8 g Protein: 6.4 g Carbs: 30 g Fiber: 8 g

132. Amaranth Tabbouleh Salad

Preparation Time: 5 minutes

Cooking Time: 10 minutes

Servings: 2

Ingredients:

- 1 small white onion, peeled and chopped
- 1 cup cooked amaranth
- ½ cucumber, deseeded, chopped
- 1 cup cooked chickpeas
- ½ medium red bell pepper, chopped

- Extra:
- ⅓ tsp sea salt
- ⅛ tsp cayenne pepper
- 2 tbsp key lime juice

Directions

Place lime juice in a small bowl, then add a pinch of salt and stir for a few seconds until blended.

Place the remaining ingredients in a salad bowl and moisten well with the lime juice mixture, toss until blended, and finally serve.mixed and then serve.

Nutrition

Nutrition: Calories: 214, Fat: 4.5 g Protein: 6.5 g Carbs: 37 g Fiber: 9 g

133. Zucchini and Mushroom Bowl

Preparation Time: 5 minutes

Cooking Time: 8 minutes

Servings: 2

Ingredients:

- 2 zucchini, spiralized
- ½ medium red bell pepper, sliced
- ½ cup sliced mushrooms
- ½ medium green bell pepper, sliced
- ½ medium white onion, peeled, sliced
-
- Extra:
- ⅓ tsp salt

- ⅛ tsp cayenne pepper
- 1 tbsp grapeseed oil

Directions

Take a large skillet pan, place it over medium-high heat, add oil, and when hot, add onion, mushrooms, and bell peppers, and then cook for 3 to 5 minutes until tender-crisp.

Add zucchini noodles, toss until mixed, and then cook for 2 minutes until warm.

Nutrition

Nutrition: Calories: 168, Fat: 2 g Protein: 0.9 g Carbs: 36 g Fiber: 6 g

134. Pear & Strawberry Salad

Preparation Time: 15 minutes

Cooking Time: 0 minutes

Servings: 4

Ingredients:

- 4 cups romaine lettuce, torn
- 2 pears, cored and sliced
- 1 cup fresh strawberries, hulled and sliced
- ¼ cup walnuts, chopped
- 3 tbsp olive oil
- 2 tbsp fresh key lime juice
- 1 tbsp agave nectar

Directions

In a salad bowl, place all ingredients and toss to coat well.

Serve immediately.

Nutrition

Nutrition: Calories: 8, Fat: 1.8 g, Cholesterol: 0 mg, Carbs: 25.2 g, Fiber: 5.1 g, Protein: 2.8 g

135. Raspberry & Arugula Salad

Preparation Time: 15 minutes

Cooking Time: 0 minutes

Servings: 2

Ingredients:

- Salad
- 3 cups fresh baby arugula
- 1 cup fresh raspberries
- ¼ cup walnuts, chopped
- Dressing:
- 1 tbsp olive oil
- 1 tbsp fresh key lime juice
- ½ tsp agave nectar
- Sea salt, as needed

Directions

For the salad: Place all ingredients in a salad bowl and mix.

For the dressing: Place all ingredients in another bowl and beat until well combined.

Pour the dressing over the salad and toss to coat well.

Serve immediately.

Nutrition

Nutrition: Calories: 202, Fat: 1.6 g Cholesterol: 0 mg Carbs: 11.4 g Fiber: 5.6 g Protein: 5.3 g

136. Mixed Berries Salad

Preparation Time: 15 minutes

Cooking Time: 15 minutes

Servings: 4

Ingredients:

- 1 cup fresh strawberries, hulled and sliced
- ½ cup fresh blackberries
- ½ cup fresh blueberries
- ½ cup fresh raspberries
- 6 cups fresh arugula
- 2 tbsp olive oil
- Sea salt, as needed

 **Directions**

In a salad bowl, place all ingredients and toss to coat well.

Serve immediately.

 **Nutrition**

Nutrition: Calories: 105, Fat: 1 g Cholesterol: 0 mg Carbs: 10.1 g Fiber: 3.6 g Protein: 1.6 g

137. Apple & Kale Salad

Preparation Time: 15 minutes

Cooking Time: 15 minutes

Servings: 4

Ingredients:

- 3 large apples, cored and sliced
- 6 cups fresh baby kale
- ¼ cup walnuts, chopped
- 2 tbsp olive oil
- 1 tbsp agave nectar
- Sea salt, as needed

 **Directions**

In a salad bowl, place all ingredients and toss to coat well.

Serve immediately.

 **Nutrition**

Nutrition: Calories: 260, Fat: 1.3 g Cholesterol: 0 mg Carbs: 38.4 g Fiber: 6.3 g Protein: 5.3 g

138. Mango & Arugula Salad

Preparation Time: 15 minutes

Cooking Time: 15 minutes

Servings: 6

Ingredients:

- 2 ½ cups mangoes; peeled, pitted and sliced
- 2 ½ cups avocados; peeled, pitted and sliced
- 1 red onion, sliced
- 6 cups fresh baby arugula
- ¼ cup fresh mint leaves, chopped
- 2 tbsp fresh orange juice
- Sea salt, as needed

 **Directions**

Place all ingredients in a salad bowl and gently toss to combine.

Cover and refrigerate to chill before serving.

 **Nutrition**

Nutrition: Calories: 182, Fat: 2.6 g Cholesterol: 0 mg Carbs: 18.8 g Fiber: 6.2 g Protein: 2.6 g

139. Orange & Kale Salad

Preparation Time: 10 minutes

Cooking Time: 10 minutes

Servings: 2

Ingredients:

Salad:

- 3 cups fresh kale, tough ribs removed and torn
- 2 oranges, peeled and segmented
- 2 tbsp fresh cranberries
-
- Dressing:
- 2 tbsp olive oil
- 2 tbsp fresh orange juice
- ½ tsp agave nectar
- Sea salt, as needed

Directions

For the salad: Place all ingredients in a salad bowl and mix.

For the dressing: Place all ingredients in n another bowl and beat until well combined.

Pour the dressing over the salad and toss to coat well.

Serve immediately.

Nutrition

Nutrition: Calories: 272, Fat: 2 g Cholesterol: 0 mg Carbs: 35.7 g Fiber: 6.3 g Protein: 4.8 g

140. Aloe & Tomato Salad

Preparation Time: 15 minutes

Cooking Time: 15 minutes

Servings: 4

Ingredients:

- 2 medium Aloe, sliced
- 2 cups plum tomatoes, sliced
- 2 tbsp olive oil
- 2 tbsp fresh key lime juice
- Pinch sea salt

Directions

In a salad bowl, place all ingredients and gently toss to combine.

Serve immediately.

Nutrition

Nutrition: Calories: 93, Fat: 1.1 g Cholesterol: 0 mg Carbs: 6.9 g Fiber: 2.2 g Protein: 2 g

141. Tomato & Arugula Salad

Preparation Time: 15 minutes

Cooking Time: 15 minutes

Servings: 4

Ingredients:

- 6 cups fresh baby arugula
- 2 cups cherry tomatoes
- 2 scallions, chopped
- 2 tbsp olive oil
- 2 tbsp fresh orange juice
- Sea salt, as needed

 **Directions**

In a salad bowl, place all ingredients and toss to combine.

Cover the bowl and refrigerate for about 6–8 hours.

Remove from the refrigerator and toss well before serving.

 **Nutrition**

Nutrition: Calories: 90, Fat: 1.1 g Cholesterol: 0 mg Carbs: 6 g Fiber: 1.8 g Protein: 1.8 g

142. Warm Avo and Quinoa Salad

Preparation Time: 5 minutes

Cooking Time: 12 minutes

Servings: 4

Ingredients:

- 4 ripe avocados, quartered
- 1 cup quinoa
- 0.9 lb Chickpeas, drained
- 1 oz flat-leaf parsley

 **Directions**

Add quinoa to a pot with 2 cups of water. Bring to boil then simmer for 12 minutes or until all the water has evaporated. The grains should be glassy and swollen.

Toss the quinoa with all other ingredients and season with salt and pepper to taste.

Serve with olive oil and lemon wedges. Enjoy.

 **Nutrition**

Nutrition: Calories: 354, Fat: 16 g Carbs: 31 g Protein: 15 g Fiber: 15 g

143. Chickpeas & Quinoa Salad

Preparation Time: 20 minutes

Cooking Time: 20 minutes

Servings: 8

Ingredients:

- 1 ¾ cup spring water
- 1 cup quinoa, rinsed
- Sea salt, as needed
- 2 cups cooked chickpeas
- 1 medium red bell pepper, seeded and chopped
- 1 medium green bell pepper, seeded and chopped
- 2 large cucumbers, chopped
- ½ cup onion, chopped
- 3 tbsp olive oil
- 4 tbsp fresh basil leaves, chopped

Directions

In a pan, add the water over high heat and bring it to boil.

Add the quinoa and salt and cook until boiling.

Now, adjust the heat to low and simmer, covering for about 15–20 minutes or until all the liquid is absorbed.

Remove from the heat and set aside, covering for about 5–10 minutes.

Uncover and with a fork, fluff the quinoa.

In a salad bowl, place quinoa with the remaining ingredients and gently toss to coat.

Serve immediately.

Nutrition

Nutrition: Calories: 215, Fat: 1 g Cholesterol: 0 mg Carbs: 30.5 g Fiber: 5.6 g Protein: 7.5 g

144. Quinoa, Tomato & Mango Salad

Preparation Time: 15 minutes

Cooking Time: 0 minutes

Servings: 4

Ingredients:

- 2 cups mango; peeled, pitted and chopped
- 1 cup cooked quinoa
- 1 green bell pepper, seeded and chopped
- 1 cup cherry tomato, halved
- ½ cup fresh parsley, chopped
- ¼ cup onion, sliced
- 2 garlic cloves, minced
- 2 tbsp fresh key lime juice
- 1 ½ tbsp olive oil
- Pinch sea salt

Directions

In a salad bowl, place all ingredients and gently stir to combine.

Refrigerate for about 1–2 hours before serving.

Nutrition

Nutrition: Calories: 270, Fat: 1.2 g Cholesterol: 0 mg Carbs: 45.3 g Fiber: 5.7 g Protein: 7.8 g

Chapter 10. Juices and Smoothies

145. Apple and Avocado Smoothie

Preparation Time: 5 minutes

Cooking Time: 0 minutes

Servings: 2

Ingredients:

- 2 apples, peeled, cored, diced
- 4 cups Kale leaves
- 1 avocado, peeled, pitted
- 1 burro banana, peeled
- 2 tsp agave syrup
-
- Extra:
- 1 cup walnut milk, unsweetened

 **Directions**

Plug in a high-speed food processor or blender and add all the ingredients to its jar.

Cover the blender jar with its lid and then pulse for 40 to 60 seconds until smooth.

Divide the drink between 2 glasses and then serve.

 **Nutrition**

Nutrition: Calories: 216.4 Fat: 7.5 g Protein: 2.9 g Carbs: 39.3 g Fiber: 7.7 g

146. Key Lime Tea

Preparation Time: 5 minutes

Cooking Time: 10 minutes

Servings: 2

Ingredients:

- 1 sprig dill weed
- 1/16 tsp cayenne pepper
- 1 tbsp key lime juice
- 2 cups spring water

 **Directions**

Take a medium saucepan, place it over medium-high heat, pour in water, and then bring it to a boil.

Boil for 5 minutes, and then strain the tea into a bowl.

Add lime juice stir until mixed and then stir in cayenne pepper.

Divide tea between 2 mugs and then serve.

 **Nutrition**

Nutrition: Calories: 2.4, Fat: 0 g Protein: 0 g Carbs: 0.5 g Fiber: 0 g

147. Kale and Apple Smoothie

Preparation Time: 5 minutes

Cooking Time: 0 minutes

Servings: 2

Ingredients:

- 2 cups kale leaves
- 2 tbsp agave syrup
- 2 small apples, peeled, cored, diced
- 2 tbsp key lime juice
- 1 cup walnut milk, homemade

Directions

Plug in a high-speed food processor or blender and add all the ingredients to its jar.

Cover the blender jar with its lid and then pulse for 40 to 60 seconds until smooth.

Divide the drink between 2 glasses and then serve.

Nutrition

Nutrition: Calories: 121, Fat: 3.4 g Protein: 4.2 g Carbs: 22 g Fiber: 6 g

148. Amazing Sea Moss Green Drink

Preparation Time: 5 minutes

Cooking Time: 0 minutes

Servings: 2

Ingredients:

- 4 tbsp sea moss gel
- 4 cups mixed greens
- 2 burro bananas, peeled

Directions

Plug in a high-speed food processor or blender and add all the ingredients to its jar.

Cover the blender jar with its lid and then pulse for 40 to 60 seconds until smooth.

Divide the drink between 2 glasses and then serve.

Nutrition

Nutrition: Calories: 120, Fat: 0.1 g Protein: 3.4 g Carbs: 26 g Fiber: 3.4 g

149. Ki-Ki Mango & Banana Smoothie

Preparation Time: 5 minutes

Cooking Time: 0 minutes

Servings: 2

Ingredients:

- 2 cups mango pieces
- 2 burro bananas, peeled
- 2 oranges, peeled
- 2 tsp agave syrup
- ⅓ cup walnut milk, homemade

Directions

Plug in a high-speed food processor or blender and add all the ingredients to its jar.

Cover the blender jar with its lid and then pulse for 40 to 60 seconds until smooth.

Divide the drink between 2 glasses and then serve.

Nutrition

Nutrition: Calories: 157, Fat: 2 g Protein: 3 g Carbs: 35.5 g Fiber: 3.5 g

150. Orange and Lettuce Smoothie

Preparation Time: 5 minutes

Cooking Time: 0 minutes

Servings: 2

Ingredients:

- 2 oranges, peeled and sliced
- 1 cup shredded lettuce, rinsed
- 2 apples, cored, sliced
- 1 cup spring water

Directions

Plug in a high-speed food processor or blender and add all the ingredients to its jar.

Cover the blender jar with its lid and then pulse for 40 to 60 seconds until smooth.

Divide the drink between 2 glasses and then serve.

Nutrition

Nutrition: Calories: 140, Fat: 0.9 g Protein: 1.3 g Carbs: 31.8 g Fiber: 3 g

151. Green Tea and Lettuce Detox Smoothie

Preparation Time: 5 minutes

Cooking Time: 0 minutes

Servings: 2

Ingredients:

- ½ burro banana
- ¼ cup blueberries, fresh
- 1 cup Romaine lettuce
- 3 tbsp key lime juice
-
- Extra:
- ½ cup soft jelly coconut water

Directions

Plug in a high-speed food processor or blender and add all the ingredients to its jar.

Cover the blender jar with its lid and then pulse for 40 to 60 seconds until smooth.

Divide the drink between 2 glasses and then serve.

Nutrition

Nutrition: Calories: 134, Fat: 4.5 g Protein: 4.6 g Carbs: 20 g Fiber: 3.7 g

152. Chamomile Delight Smoothie

Preparation Time: 5 minutes

Cooking Time: 0 minutes

Servings: 2

Ingredients:

- 2 burro bananas, peeled
- ½ cup chamomile tea
- 1 tbsp date
- ½ cup walnut milk, homemade

Directions

Plug in a high-speed food processor or blender and add all the ingredients to its jar.

Cover the blender jar with its lid and then pulse for 40 to 60 seconds until smooth.

Divide the drink between 2 glasses and then serve.

Nutrition

Nutrition: Calories: 142, Fat: 5 g Protein: 3.5 g Carbs: 25 g Fiber: 8.5 g

153. Honey Dew and Arugula Smoothie

Preparation Time: 5 minutes

Cooking Time: 0 minutes

Servings: 2

Ingredients:

- 1 large bunch Callaloo
- 1 cup cucumber, deseeded
- 1 large bunch arugulas
- ¼ cup honeydew pieces
- 1 pear, diced
-
- Extra:
- 6 dates, pitted
- 1 tbsp of sea moss gel
- ¼ cup key lime juice
- 2 cups soft-jelly coconut water

 **Directions**

Plug in a high-speed food processor or blender and add all the ingredients to its jar.

Cover the blender jar with its lid and then pulse for 40 to 60 seconds until smooth.

Divide the drink between 2 glasses and then serve.

 **Nutrition**

Nutrition: Calories: 189.5 Fat: 2.5 g Protein: 1.5 g Carbs: 42.6 g Fiber: 6.6 g

154. Watermelon and Strawberries Drink

Preparation Time: 5 minutes

Cooking Time: 0 minutes

Servings: 2

Ingredients:

- 1 cup strawberries
- 1 cup watermelon, chunks
- 1 tsp date
- 1 cup soft jelly coconut water

 **Directions**

Plug in a high-speed food processor or blender and add all the ingredients to its jar.

Cover the blender jar with its lid and then pulse for 40 to 60 seconds until smooth.

Divide the drink between 2 glasses and then serve.

 **Nutrition**

Nutrition: Calories: 110, Fat: 0 g Protein: 0 g Carbs: 28 g Fiber: 6 g

155. Sweet Green Drink

Preparation Time: 5 minutes

Cooking Time: 10 minutes

Servings: 2

Ingredients:

- 1 cup greens
- 1 cucumber, peeled, deseeded
- 1 key lime, peeled
- 2 dates, pitted
-
- Extra:
- 2 cups of soft-jelly coconut water

Directions

Plug in a high-speed food processor or blender and add all the ingredients to its jar.

Cover the blender jar with its lid and then pulse for 40 to 60 seconds until smooth.

Divide the drink between 2 glasses and then serve.

Nutrition

Nutrition: Calories: 112, Fat: 0.1 g Protein: 0.3 g Carbs: 27 g Fiber: 5 g

156. Banana Sea Moss Smoothie

Preparation Time: 5 minutes

Cooking Time: 0 minutes

Servings: 2

Ingredients:

- 1 cup kale
- ½ apple, cored, sliced
- 1 tsp sea moss
- ½ burro banana
-
- Extra:
- 1 tsp Bromide Plus Powder

Directions

Plug in a high-speed food processor or blender and add all the ingredients to its jar.

Cover the blender jar with its lid and then pulse for 40 to 60 seconds until smooth.

Divide the drink between 2 glasses and then serve.

Nutrition

Nutrition: Calories: 115, Fat: 0.5 g Protein: 2 g Carbs: 28 g Fiber: 2 g

157. Smoothie Bowl

Preparation Time: 5 minutes

Cooking Time: 0 minutes

Servings: 2

Ingredients:

- 1 burro banana, peeled
- 1 ½ cup mixed berries
- 1 mango, peeled, destoned, chopped
- 2 tbsp walnut milk, homemade
- 1 tbsp walnut butter, homemade
-
- Extra:
- 2 tbsp agave syrup

Directions

Plug in a high-speed food processor or blender, add banana and berries, and then pulse at low speed until small pieces of fruit remain in the jar.

Add milk, butter, and agave syrup, pulse until combined, and then divide the mixture evenly between 2 bowls.

Top evenly with mango slices and some more berries and then serve.

Storage instructions:

Divide the drink between 2 jars or bottles, cover them with a lid, and then store the containers in the refrigerator for up to 3 days.

Nutrition

Nutrition: Calories: 338, Fat: 9.6 g Protein: 8.6 g Carbs: 64.3 g Fiber: 12.1 g

158. Refreshing Smoothie with Nuts

Preparation Time: 5 minutes

Cooking Time: 0 minutes

Servings: 2

Ingredients:

- ½ burro banana, peeled
- ½ cup figs
- 2 strawberries
- ¼ cup Brazil nuts
- 1 cup spring water

Directions

Plug in a high-speed food processor or blender and add all the ingredients to its jar.

Cover the blender jar with its lid and then pulse for 40 to 60 seconds until smooth.

Divide the drink between 2 glasses and then serve.

Storage instructions:

Divide the drink between 2 jars or bottles, cover them with a lid, and then store the containers in the refrigerator for up to 3 days.

Nutrition

Nutrition: Calories: 234, Fat: 2 g Protein: 6.1 g Carbs: 53.1 g Fiber: 5.8 g

159. Cantaloupe Smoothie Tea

Preparation Time: 5 minutes

Cooking Time: 0 minutes

Servings: 2

Ingredients:

- 1 cantaloupe, peeled, deseeded, sliced
- ½ cup Herbal Tea
- ½ of burro banana, peeled
- ½ cup soft-jelly coconut water

Directions

Plug in a high-speed food processor or blender and add all the ingredients to its jar.

Cover the blender jar with its lid and then pulse for 40 to 60 seconds until smooth.

Divide the drink between 2 glasses and then serve.

Storage instructions:

Divide the drink between 2 jars or bottles, cover them with a lid, and then store the containers in the refrigerator for up to 3 days.

Nutrition

Nutrition: Calories: 114.7, Fat: 0.6 g Protein: 1.8 g Carbs: 27.8 g Fiber: 1 g

160. Papaya and Quinoa Smoothie

Preparation Time: 5 minutes

Cooking Time: 10 minutes

Servings: 2

Ingredients:

- 2 cups papaya cubes
- 2 tbsp date
- 1 cup cooked quinoa or amaranth
- 2 tsp Bromide Plus Powder
- 2 cups hemp milk, homemade

Directions

Plug in a high-speed food processor or blender and add all the ingredients to its jar.

Cover the blender jar with its lid and then pulse for 40 to 60 seconds until smooth.

Divide the drink between 2 glasses and then serve

Nutrition

Nutrition: Calories: 224.6 Fat: 7.7 g Protein: 7 g Carbs: 33.7 g Fiber: 3.5 g

161. Avocado and Cucumber Smoothie

Preparation Time: 5 minutes

Cooking Time: 0 minutes

Servings: 2

Ingredients:

- 1 burro banana, peeled
- ¼ avocado
- ¼ cucumber
- 1 tbsp agave syrup
- ½ cup herbal tea
-
- Extra:
- 1 tbsp chopped walnuts
- 1 cup soft-jelly coconut milk, homemade

Directions

Plug in a high-speed food processor or blender and add all the ingredients to its jar.

Cover the blender jar with its lid and then pulse for 40 to 60 seconds until smooth.

Divide the drink between 2 glasses and then serve.

Nutrition

Nutrition: Calories: 103, Fat: 4.5 g Protein: 1.6 g Carbs: 16.2 g Fiber: 2.5 g

162. Jamaican Irish Moss Drink

Preparation Time: 5 minutes

Cooking Time: 0 minutes

Servings: 2

Ingredients:

- ½ cup raspberries
- 1 mason jar sea moss gel
- ½ cup green coconut water
- 1 tbsp date

Directions

Take out a jar of prepared sea moss gel.

Plug in a high-speed food processor or blender and add all the ingredients to its jar.

Cover the blender jar with its lid and then pulse for 40 to 60 seconds until smooth.

Divide the drink between 2 glasses and then serve.

Nutrition

Nutrition: Calories: 130, Fat: 1.5 g Protein: 5 g Carbs: 26 g Fiber: 4 g

163. Orange and Banana Drink

Preparation Time: 5 minutes

Cooking Time: 0 minutes

Servings: 2

Ingredients:

- ½ burro banana, peeled
- 3 oranges, peeled
- 1 ½ tbsp Date
- ½ tsp Bromide Plus Powder
- 1 cup of soft-jelly coconut water

Directions

Plug in a high-speed food processor or blender and add all the ingredients to its jar.

Cover the blender jar with its lid and then pulse for 40 to 60 seconds until smooth.

Divide the drink between 2 glasses and then serve.

Nutrition

Nutrition: Calories: 138.5, Fat: 0.6 g Protein: 1.5 g Carbs: 35.1 g Fiber: 4.7 g

164. Lettuce, Banana and Berries Smoothie

Preparation Time: 5 minutes

Cooking Time: 0 minutes

Servings: 2

Ingredients:

- ½ burro banana
- ¼ cup blueberries
- 1 cup Romaine lettuce
- 2 tbsp key lime juice
- ½ cup soft jelly coconut water

Directions

Plug in a high-speed food processor or blender and add all the ingredients: to its jar.

Cover the blender jar with its lid and then pulse for 40 to 60 seconds until smooth.

Divide the drink between 2 glasses and then serve.

Nutrition

Nutrition: Calories: 147, Fat: 0.8 g Protein: 3.3 g Carbs: 36 g Fiber: 4 g

165. Apple, Quinoa and Fig Smoothie

Preparation Time: 5 minutes

Cooking Time: 0 minutes

Servings: 2

Ingredients:

- ½ cup cooked quinoa
- ½ large red apple, cored
- 1 cup amaranth greens
- 1 fig
- 1 tsp Bromide Plus Powder
-
- Extra:
- 1 tbsp raisins
- 1 tbsp date
- 1 cup hemp seed milk, homemade

Directions

Plug in a high-speed food processor or blender and add all the ingredients to its jar.

Cover the blender jar with its lid and then pulse for 40 to 60 seconds until smooth.

Divide the drink between 2 glasses and then serve.

Nutrition

Nutrition: Calories: 153, Fat: 1 g Protein: 3 g Carbs: 28 g Fiber: 3 g

166. Strawberry Shake

Preparation Time: 5 minutes

Cooking Time: 10 minutes

Servings: 2

Ingredients:

- 1 cup strawberries
- ½ cup Brazil nuts, soaked
- 1 tbsp agave syrup
- ⅓ cup Irish Moss gel
- 1 ½ cup spring water

Directions

Plug in a high-speed food processor or blender and add all the ingredients to its jar.

Cover the blender jar with its lid and then pulse for 40 to 60 seconds until smooth.

Divide the drink between 2 glasses and then serve.

Nutrition

Nutrition: Calories: 137, Fat: 5 g Protein: 1 g Carbs: 22 g Fiber: 2 g

167. Sweet Sunrise Smoothie

Preparation Time: 5 minutes

Cooking Time: 0 minutes

Servings: 2

Ingredients:

- 1 cup mango chunks
- 1 cup raspberries
- ½ burro banana
- 1 orange, peeled
- 1 cup spring water

Directions

Plug in a high-speed food processor or blender and add all the ingredients to its jar.

Cover the blender jar with its lid and then pulse for 40 to 60 seconds until smooth.

Divide the drink between 2 glasses and then serve.

Nutrition

Nutrition: Calories: 130, Fat: 0 g Protein: 0 g Carbs: 30 g Fiber: 3 g

168. Green Sea Moss Drink

Preparation Time: 5 minutes

Cooking Time: 0 minutes

Servings: 2

Ingredients:

- 1 apple, cored, diced
- 2 cups kale
- 1 cup cucumber chunks
- 2 cups coconut water
-
- Extra:
- 1 key lime, juiced
- 1 tbsp sea moss gel

Directions

Plug in a high-speed food processor or blender and add all the ingredients to its jar.

Cover the blender jar with its lid and then pulse for 40 to 60 seconds until smooth.

Divide the drink between 2 glasses and then serve.

Nutrition

Nutrition: Calories: 156, Fat: 1.8 g Protein: 9.4 g Carbs: 32.8 g Fiber: 10.2 g

MEAL PLAN

DAY	BREAKFAST	LUNCH	SNACKS	DINNER
01	Farro Salad	Vegetarian Spanish Mixed Greenn Salad	Apple and Avocado Smoothie	Mushrooms Stuffed & Crab Paste
02	Chili Avocado Scramble	Vegetarian Spanish Rice Dinner	Key Lime Tea	Chicken Skewers with Peppers and Pineapple
03	Tapioca Pudding	Champinones Spanish Garlic Mushrooms	Kale and Apple Smoothie	Greek Salad Skewers
04	Cauliflower Hash Brown Breakfast Bowl	Greek Vegetarian Stuffed Zucchini	Amazing Sea Moss Green Drink	Sweet-Smelling Chicken Breast with Kale, Red Onion, And Salsa
05	Pumpkin Coconut Oatmeal	Greek Vegetarian Soutzoukakia	Ki-Ki Mango & Banana Smoothie	Tuscan Bean Stew
06	Bacon, Vegetable and Parmesan Combo	Lean and Green "Macaroni	Orange and Lettuce Smoothie	Fragrant Asian Hotpot
07	Toasted Crostini	Lean and Green Broccoli Taco	Green Tea and Lettuce Detox Smoothie	Chicken Fry with Peanut Sauce

NOTE

MEAL PLAN

DAY	BREAKFAST	LUNCH	SNACKS	DINNER
08	Heavenly Egg Bake with Blackberry	Lean and Green Crunchy Chicken Tacos	Chamomile Delight Smoothie	Chicken Cacciatore
09	Quick Cream of Wheat	Cauliflower with Kale Pesto	Honey Dew and Arugula Smoothie	Toasted Sardines
10	Feta And Eggs Mix	Lean and Green Chicken Chili	Watermelon and Strawberries Drink	Savory Crêpes with Vegetables
11	Banana Pancakes	Lean and Green Broccoli Alfredo	Sweet Green Drink	Fusilli Pasta With Cherry Tomatoes, Capers and Crunchy Crumbs
12	Nectarine Pancakes	Lean and Green Steak Machine	Banana Sea Moss Smoothie	Pan- cooked Aubergine Olives and Capers
13	Raspberry Pudding	Lean and Green Crockpot Chili	Smoothie Bow	Avocado Lime Shrimp Salad
14	Detox Porridge	Buffalo Cauliflower Bites	Refreshing Smoothie with Nuts	Rosemary Cauliflower Rolls

NOTE

MEAL PLAN

DAY	BREAKFAST	LUNCH	SNACKS	DINNER
15	Avocado Crab Omelet	Lovely Faux Mac and Cheese	Cantaloupe Smoothie Tea	Delicious Lemon Chicken Salad
16	Buckwheat Pancakes	Greek Steamed Vegetable Bowls	Papaya and Quinoa Smoothie	Healthy Chicken Orzo
17	Apple Oatmeal	Greek Veggie Balls with Tahini Lemon Sauce	Avocado and Cucumber Smoothie	Lemon Garlic Chicken
18	Raspberry Overnight Porridge	Briam Greek Roasted Vegetables	Jamaican Irish Moss Drink	Chicken Cacciatore
19	Cheesy Scrambled Eggs with Fresh Herbs	Yemista (Stuffed Peppers and Tomatoes)	Orange and Banana Drink	Fennel Wild Rice Risotto
20	Turkey and Spinach Scramble on Melba Toast	Greek Vegetarian Meatballs	Lettuce, Banana and Berries Smoothie	Wild Rice Prawn Salad
21	Vegetable Omelet	Greek Lasagna Vegetarian	Apple, Quinoa and Fig Smoothie	King Prawn Stirfry & Soba

NOTE

MEAL PLAN

DAY	BREAKFAST	LUNCH	SNACKS	DINNER
22	Walnuts Yogurt Mix	Greek Style Baked Feta	Strawberry Shake	Baked Potatoes with Spicy Chickpea Stew
23	Mediterranean Eggfeta Scramble	Chicken Stir Fry	Sweet Sunrise Smoothie	Kale and Red Onion Dhal with Buckwheat
24	Spiced Chickpeas Bowls	Lean and Green Garlic Chicken with Zoodles	Green Sea Moss Drink	Date and Walnut Cinnamon Bites
25	Orzo And Veggie Bowls	Vegetarian cooked Chorizo with Chick Peas and Tomatoes	Apple and Avocado Smoothie	Chicken Casserole
26	Vanilla Oats	Mediterranean Spanish Roasted Vegetables	Key Lime Tea	Mushrooms Stuffed & Crab Paste
27	Mushroom-Egg Casserole	Tapas & Pinchos Vegetarian	Kale and Apple Smoothie	Chicken Skewers with Peppers and Pineapple
28	Bacon Veggies Combo	Vegetarian Spanish Toast with Escalivada	Amazing Sea Moss Green Drink	Greek Salad Skewers

NOTE

MEAL PLAN

DAY	BREAKFAST	LUNCH	SNACKS	DINNER
29	Brown Rice Salad	Vegetarian Garlic Soup with Egg and Croutons	Ki-Ki Mango & Banana Smoothie	Sweet-Smelling Chicken Breast with Kale, Red Onion, And Salsa
30	Olive And Milk Bread	Mediterranean Baked Vegetarian Tapas	Orange and Lettuce Smoothie	Tuscan Bean Stew

NOTE

GLYCEMIC INDEX
Low GI (<55), Mewdium GI (56-69) and High GI (70>)

Grains/ Starchs		Vegetables		Fruits		Dairy		Protein	
Rice Bran	27	Asparagus	15	Grapefruit	25	Low fat Yogurt	14	Beans, Dried	40
Bran Cereal	42	Broccoll	15	Apple	38	Plain Yogurt	14	Black Eyed Beans	59
Spaghetti	42	Celery	15	Peach	42	Whole Milk	27	Kidney Beans	41
Corn, Sweet	54	Cucumber	15	Orange	44	Soy Milk	32	Lentils	41
Wild Rice	57	Lettuce	15	Grape	46	Fat Free Milk	32	Lima Beans	46
Sweet Potatoes	61	Peppers	15	Banana	54	Skim Milk	33	Peanuts	21
White Rice	64	Spinach	15	Mango	56	Chocolate Milk	35	Pinto Beans	55
Cocus Cocus	65	Tomatoes	15	Pineapple	66	Fruit Yogurt	36	Split Peas	45
Whole Wheat	71	Chickpeas	33	Watermelon	72	Ice Cream	61		
Bread		Coocked Carrotes	39	Cherries	22	Soy Milk	30		
Muesli	80	Peas	22	Plums	24	Low Fat Yogurt no sugar	15		
Baked Potatoes	85	Sweet Corn	55	Kiwifruit	52	Fat Free Milk	32		
Oatmeall	87	Mashed Potato	73	Pears	36				
Taco Shells	97			Dates	100				
White Bread	100								
Bagel, White	103								
Cornflakes	84								
Banana Bread	100								
All Bran	42								
Oat Bran Bread	48								

Fatty Liver Disease

Fatty liver disease is a complication caused by excessive fat deposition in the liver cells. The liver is the second largest organ in the human body and this fat deposition can cause a lot of health problems. If not treated properly, fatty liver disease can lead to many diseases, including diabetes, high blood pressure, kidney disease, cirrhosis of the liver and liver failure. The liver contributes to carbohydrate, protein and lipid metabolism, stores energy, determines blood sugar and cholesterol levels, filters toxins from the body, fights disease and infection, contributes to body temperature regulation and acts as a blood storage organ. Among the functions performed by the liver are the storage of materials and the synthesis of plasma proteins, although it primarily serves as the body's detoxification organ. Liver disease can therefore have a serious effect on our health.

The presence of fat in the liver is a normal condition, but the presence of more than 5%-10% of fat is called fatty liver disease. Consuming high-fat foods is one of the main reasons for this. As a result of consuming more fats than the body can digest, fatty deposits occur in the liver.

Alcoholic Fatty Liver Disease (AFLD)

Drinking too much alcohol is one cause of increased fatty liver. Every time alcohol is filtered through the liver, a number of liver cells die. Whilst the liver is a self-repairing organ, heavy drinking destroys this regenerative power, resulting in more serious and permanent liver damage.

Non-Alcoholic Fatty Liver Disease (NAFLD)

Even if a person does not use alcohol, fatty deposits in the liver can still result from factors such as obesity, the use of various drugs, aging, high blood pressure, metabolic problems, rapid weight gain, high blood fat levels and viral infections such as hepatitis C or genetic diseases. The percentage of victims of this disease is increasing now.

Symptoms of this Disease

It is usually difficult to recognize the symptoms of this disease. However, some people may experience symptoms such as abdominal pain or discomfort, fatigue, loss of appetite and feeling unwell. In addition to this, symptoms such as yellowing of the eyes and skin, swelling of the ankles and abdomen, sleepiness, confusion, bleeding with vomiting, and bleeding with stool can also be the result of fatty liver disease. To confirm it, however, it is essential to go to a doctor and get a proper health checkup.

Treatment

Fatty liver disease requires natural Ayurvedic remedies because Western medicine has not yet found a cure for this disease. Doctors say that if detected in the early stages, this medical condition can be remedied because the liver regenerates itself naturally. Making favorable changes in your lifestyle as well as employing certain Ayurvedic methods can help prevent this condition. If not treated in time, however, it can lead to serious complications such as cirrhosis and multisystem disorders.

Liver disease develops slowly, so it is important for you to take steps to help prevent or treat liver problems as soon as possible. Whether you choose to use Ayurvedic remedies or drugs to improve liver function, it is important to be consistent and disciplined, as the benefits of these approaches add up over time.

Making the following lifestyle changes can reduce the severity of the disease:

➤ If you are an alcoholic, follow the steps to abstain completely from alcohol.

➤ Take care to maintain a stable body weight and prevent obesity by exercising daily. Exercise at least 45 minutes a day.

➤ Prioritize good sleep to allow enough rest for your liver and whole body to recover.

➤ If you have diabetes, try your best to control your blood sugar levels.

➤ Take all necessary steps to keep your cholesterol and triglycerides at healthy levels.

➤ If you are a sedentary person and do the same job, make sure to change your lifestyle.

➤ Eat and sleep on time. Avoid sleeping during the daytime.

➤ Keep your mind healthy. Yoga exercises can be used for this.

The health habits above will protect you not only from fatty liver disease, but also from other disease conditions.

Ayurvedic Treatment for Fatty Liver Disease

Ayurveda, a Sanskrit word for 'the knowledge of life' or 'the science of holistic health', is a system of medicine with an emphasis on disease prevention and health promotion. Ayurveda represents many of the oldest medicines in healthcare to remedy human diseases. Ayurvedic remedies have historically been considered the most powerful means of maintaining health and homeostasis.

It is believed that Ayurvedic treatments are more effective than other treatments to prevent fatty liver disease. Besides changing one's lifestyle, following Ayurvedic methods can also help one recover from this disease without side effects. Ayurvedic medicine has a history stretching back to the Stone Age. No matter how advanced the medical science has become, Ayurvedic methods remain popular because they provide tangible results. And there are many Ayurvedic methods for this condition.

Ayurvedic treatment for fatty liver begins with removing toxins from the body. Only then can other medicines work properly.

- *In alcoholic liver disease, Ayurvedic treatment reduces the toxic effects of alcohol. It deeply cleans the toxins in the liver tissue and ultimately strengthens the liver.*

- *The main cause of non-alcoholic fatty liver disease is overeating. Excessive food consumption causes toxins from undigested food to accumulate in the stomach and liver, so Ayurvedic treatment increases digestive power.*

Ayurvedic Tips to Prevent Fatty Liver Disease

  o Eat a healthy plant-based diet rich in fruits, vegetables, whole grains and healthy fats. Eat more fiber-rich foods. Most fruits are high in sugar, though, so consume fruit in moderation.
  o Eat foods rich in omega-3 fatty acids such as:
    - *Fish and other seafood (especially cold-water fatty fish, such as salmon, mackerel, tuna, herring and sardines)*
    - *Nuts and seeds (such as flaxseed, chia seeds and walnuts)*
    - *Plant oils (such as flaxseed oil, soybean oil and canola oil)*
  o Eat detoxifying and liver-restoring foods like broccoli, cabbage, cauliflower, lime, beets and cabbage.
  o Try to steam your vegetables to retain their nutritional value whilst cooking.

- o Avoid deep-fried foods and fatty meats.
- o Drink enough water, aiming for 1-2 liters per day.
- o Take probiotic supplements.
- o Eat more foods like red rice, green beans, pomegranate, dry fruits, garlic, snake gourd, coriander, bitter gourd, ginger, butter, barley, orange, raisins and drumsticks.

> ➢ *Home Remedies as Ayurvedic Treatment*

Ayurvedic quality herbal medicines can be used for certain treatments at home. However, if you are using Western medicine, it is advised to try these remedies only on medical advice. It is also advisable to seek Ayurvedic medical advice if you have any allergies.

- • *Milk Thistle*

Known as a liver tonic in recent years, milk thistle has been shown to reduce liver inflammation. Due to its non-toxic nature, it can take a long time.

- • *Turmeric*

Turmeric is a drug rich in antioxidant capabilities. Studies have shown that turmeric extract is so powerful that it protects against liver injury and protects your liver from damage caused by toxins. It can be used by people taking strong medications for diabetes or other health conditions that damage their liver with long-term use.

- • *Vegetables*

Eating beans, green vegetables (especially bitter lettuce) and from the cabbage family is another effective solution. Green leafy vegetables are also high in chlorophyll, which helps remove toxins from the bloodstream. Include one vegetable from the above daily.

- • *Aloe Vera*

Aloe vera juice is best for the liver because it is rich in hydration and phytonutrients. It is a very thick liquid made from aloe vera leaves. Staying hydrated provides a way to flush out toxins and waste from the body. It serves to reduce liver stress and is one of the best Ayurvedic treatments for fatty liver. Wash the aloe vera and make it into a juice to drink once in day.

- *Phyllanthus niruri (Bhumi-Amla)*

A plant extract called Bhumi Amla can be taken for fatty liver. This entire plant has medicinal properties. Bhumi Amla is good for indigestion and the acidity balancing of your stomach. You can take 2-4 teaspoons of Bhumi Amla juice daily. It is one of the best Ayurvedic remedies for fatty liver, with proven antioxidant and antiviral action.

- *Triphala Juice:*

Triphala is a multifunctional medicine composed of the dried fruits of the three plant species native to the Indian subcontinent Emblica officinalis, Terminalia bellerica and Terminalia chebula. It is widely used in Ayurvedic medicine as it promotes longevity and rejuvenation. Triphala juice is used as an Ayurvedic treatment for fatty liver because it helps regulate metabolism and bowel movements. Triphala is an excellent digestive remedy for the liver, as it reduces the toxic load on the liver and is a source of antioxidants that protect the liver.

- *Hogweed (Punarnava)*

In Sanskrit, Punarnava means 'to bring back to life'. It is a small plant that bears small flowers and fruits. Punarnava is highly regarded in Ayurveda as a medicinal herb for kidney disease. However, its powerful detoxifying and cleansing effects make it one of the best Ayurvedic herbs for fatty liver and other liver diseases.

- *Nuts*

Nuts rich in fat and nutrients are good for the body. Studies show that eating nuts can improve liver enzyme levels. Regular consumption of walnuts helps with liver detoxification because they contain amino acids. They also provide high levels of glutathione and omega-3 fatty acids. It has been proven that eating walnuts can improve liver function. Almonds are also rich in vitamins that help the liver. One of the simplest tips for a healthy liver is to make sure you only eat a handful a day to support your Ayurvedic treatment for fatty liver.

- *Garlic*

Garlic is available as an Ayurvedic treatment for fatty liver. Antibacterial agents and selenium from garlic help the liver naturally remove toxins from the body. As you can find this very easily, you can have two cloves of garlic every night before going to bed to help detoxify the liver.

- ***Fruits, Whole Grains, Fresh Milk***

Eating sweet fruits, whole grains (especially oats and barley) and fresh milk (in moderation) are great for liver detoxification. Make sure your diet includes grapes, apples, avocados and citrus fruits. These fruits are good for the intestines and have a stimulating effect on the liver. Rich in fiber, whole grain products such as oatmeal, brown rice, millet and barley are good choices, as they can improve blood sugar and lipid regulation. Milk because of its whey protein helps protect the liver from further damage.

- ***Kalmegh***

Kalmegh, a plant also known as the 'king of bitters', is one of the best herbal ingredients to protect the liver and treat fatty liver problems. You can consume Kalmegh in supplement form or look for Ayurvedic liver medicines that include it as a key ingredient. Kalmegh is extremely effective as a liver protector because of the phytochemicals found in the herb called *Diterpene labdanes*. Studies have shown that these exhibit potent antioxidant, liver-protecting properties.

- ***Indian Bedellium (Guggulu)***

Guggulu, commonly known as Indian bedellium, is one of the most widely used herbs in Ayurveda. The name Guggulu means that the plant protects the body from many diseases. It is also widely used herbal supplement and is finally also used in many Ayurvedic recipes as an important ingredient for fatty liver disease. The herb or gum is effective in promoting liver health due to the presence of a phytosteroid called guggulsterone. Research has shown that this phytosteroid lowers free fatty acids in the serum and liver.

- ***Neem***

Neem is one of the most popular and easily accessible herbs across most of the country, with a long history of use in Ayurveda. You can enjoy the health benefits of neem by using neem leaves to make your own herbal tea. Neem is also a common ingredient in some of the most effective natural remedies for fatty liver disease, as it improves your digestion and metabolism. Evidence from studies has proven the hepatoprotective effects of neem: reducing the accumulation of fatty tissue in the liver and promoting liver function. Diluted neem extract taken 20-30 minutes before a meal supports liver function, detoxification and digestion.

- *Kutki*

Botanically classified as *Picrorhiza kurroa*, kutki is known as a detoxifying, anti-inflammatory and antioxidant ayurvedic plant. You can buy it in powder form, but it is best consumed in combination with other hepatoprotective herbs such as guggulu and kalmegh, so it makes sense to look into herbal liver supplements that contain this herb.

- *Bitter Gourd*

Bitter gourd is considered an effective natural treatment for fatty liver and other liver disorders, and studies show that it can reverse fatty deposits in the liver and reduce liver lipid levels. You can consume it as a juice or as a vegetable dish. If you add it into your diet once a week, it will be more effective for reducing fatty liver complications.

Yoga for Fatty Liver Disease

Yoga can be described as a form of exercise that provides physical and mental health benefits for people of all ages. Although it is designed as a form of exercise, it is also a breathing exercise. Whether you are dealing with an illness, recovering from surgery, or living with a chronic condition, it is important to make yoga an integral part of your treatment. It can help you recover quickly.

Yoga is the most effective and natural exercise to keep your liver healthy. Certain asanas in yoga improve liver health by increasing liver enzyme activity. These exercises also help to increase the function of your spleen. Because yoga puts pressure on the entire liver, it strengthens your liver and thereby improves your liver function. Certain yoga postures even evaporate fatty deposits in the liver. By increasing the supply of oxygenated blood to the body, yoga helps to kill pathogenic bacteria. Both lipid metabolism and insulin production are also increased by yoga.

Below are some yoga asanas that can help alleviate liver-related problems:

- *Kapalbhati Pranayama*

This is a breathing exercise that helps to stimulate the liver and increase its function.

Sit cross-legged. Breathe in deeply and exhale through the nostrils. Remain focused on breathing. Sit comfortably so that your spine is upright. Rest your hands on your knees with palms open toward the sky and inhale deeply. When you exhale, pull your belly button inward and your spine back. If you want, you can also hold your right hand on your stomach to feel your abdominal muscles contract. Take 20 such breaths to complete one round of Kapal Bhati Pranayama. After completing one round, relax with your eyes closed and observe the sensations in your body. Then do two more rounds of Kapal Bhati Pranayama.

- **Fish Pose**

This yoga pose helps stimulate and strengthen the liver.

Sit cross-legged and cross your left leg over your right leg. Make sure the knees are lifted off the ground and pointed upwards. Hold your left leg by moving your right hand over your left leg. As you turn your head to the right, press your left foot towards your abdomen.

- **Bow Pose**

This yoga pose helps to strengthen and stretch the liver.

Lie on your stomach on your mat, with a blanket under your pelvis if needed. Now push all your toes to the floor and then bend your knees, keeping your toes active. Grasp the outer edges of your ankles and flex your feet firmly. As you exhale, lift the rib cage and shoulders toward the ears. Then extend the tailbone and push the legs back toward the hands. Now raise your head and chest. Looking down press through the thighs to lift the chest. Remain lifted for 5 breaths.

Cow Face Pose

This pose aids blood circulation in the liver and improves the metabolism of fat deposits.

Begin by sitting with one leg crossed over the other. Lengthen your spine and extend your arms behind you so that one hand is over your ribcage and the other is over your shoulder. Hold hands and try to hold the pose for as long as you can.

- *Boat Pose*

This yoga pose helps to remove harmful toxins from the liver.

Begin by lying on your back. Try to lift your chest and your legs up at the same time and put your weight on the buttocks. Inhale and exhale slowly and deeply. Try to hold the pose for as long as you can. Then return to the starting position and repeat.

- *Plow Pose*

Plow pose helps reduce your fatigue, improve your blood circulation and boost your metabolism. This pose also supports your liver in its detoxification activities. On top of that, it improves your heart function, which plays an important role in the health of your liver.

Lie on your back and keep your legs together. Lift your body and legs up into an inverted upright position. Get into a shoulder stand, balancing inverted pose on your shoulders. Support your hips with your hands, bend your legs at your hips and slowly lower them over your head. Bring your legs down so that you can touch the floor above your head with your toes. Breathe steadily and hold the pose for 5-7 breaths.

As you bend your legs down, your knees will tend to bend and extend outward. You have to resist this. If the pose seems awkward, lower your legs partially at first. Then let your hips drop a little, but hold them in your hands. Then increase your hip flexion and push your hips up with your hands.

- *Downward-Facing Dog*

Downward-facing dog pose helps your body's cells to store nutrients, including fat, which counteracts the effects of insulin resistance. This pose greatly benefits your hormonal activity, which strengthens your liver health. In a holistic sense, it will improve all of your body's major systems, including the nervous, cardiovascular and metabolic systems.

Get down on your knees and hands. Keep your knees hip-width apart and below your hips. Keep your wrists below your shoulders. Lift your knees up and push your buttocks up and back, straightening both your arms and legs. Keep pushing your buttocks up and back so that you can stretch your arms and upper back, then push your chest down and plant your heels back onto the floor. Do not bend your knees. Hold the pose for 5 breaths and repeat three times.

To add a lunge-specific movement, you can add a harness to your downward dog. Whilst holding it, twist your torso to your right to grasp the left leg with your right hand. Then twist your left leg to your left side to hold it with your right hand.

Conclusion

Welcome to the Fatty Liver Cookbook. This book contains a collection of recipes for using fatty liver as a cooking ingredient. In this book, you'll find an assortment of both savory and sweet dishes that are sure to tantalize your taste buds and your body.

Fatty liver is commonly found in beef, pork, and poultry meat but can be substituted with other proteins if not available or desired due to high prices associated with fatty liver being much more expensive than other cuts. It is safe to eat when cooked at low temperatures because it does contain small amounts of connective tissue which may make some people uncomfortable but shouldn't cause negative side effects or contraindications when eaten in moderation.

In this book, we've created recipes that are not only healthy but tasty and enjoyable to eat. They are intended to be an appetizer or side dish for your main course, but they can also be served as a main course on their own. No matter how you eat it, our recipes will make you feel good!

For those readers who wish to substitute the fatty liver with other types of protein organs, please keep in mind that the amount of connective tissue required to make a dish healthy as presented in this book is extremely small. Most fatty liver is needed only for its nutritional benefits and shouldn't be discounted because of certain food allergies or intolerances.

If you have any questions or comments, please feel free to add them in the section below. We love to hear from our readers!

Thank you.

Printed in Great Britain
by Amazon

25006066R00084